SOLVE
The Secret Sauce for 1 X 1s

SUNIL GEORGE

STARDOM BOOKS

STARDOM BOOKS

WORLDWIDE

www.StardomBooks.com

STARDOM BOOKS

A Division of Stardom Publishing

and infoYOGIS Technologies.

105-501 Silverside Road

Wilmington, DE 19809

FIRST EDITION FEBRUARY 2019

Stardom Books

SOLVE

The Secret Sauce for 1 X 1s

Sunil George

p. 150
cm. 21.5 x 13.9

Category: Self-Help/
Professional Training & Coaching

ISBN-13: 978-1-7323287-8-5

ISBN-10: 1-7323287-8-1

DEDICATION

To my dearest children Kevin and Karen –
Always be the best you can be!
– Dad

CONTENTS

PART ONE – UNDERSTANDING SOLVE   1

Big Idea 1: We Can All **'Help'** Someone   1

PART TWO - THE MODEL   3

Big Idea 2: Solve© A Thumb-Rule For **Coaching** And **Consulting**   3

Big Idea 3: Seek The Data, Find Out The Story Behind The Numbers   9

Big Idea 4: Observe, Define The **Outcome** And The Real Need Behind The Need   23

Big Idea 5 – Be A Reflective **Listen**er   43

Big Idea 6 – When You **Value-Add**, Create Insights, Get The Client To Think New Solutions   57

Big Idea 7 – Ensure You **Evaluate**. What You Inspect, They Respect.   73

PART THREE - APPLICATION AND TIPS   89

Big Idea 8 - Solve© In Coaching – Measure And
Monitor Change   89

Big Idea 9 - Solve© In Consulting – Right People
Matter   107

Big Idea 10 - Solve© Requires A Culture Shift. It Is
About A Mindset   123

CHAPTER OUTLINE AND OVERVIEW   **135**

ACKNOWLEDGMENTS

To the almighty for inspiring me in all I do. To my Dad and Mom for all that I am today.

My loving wife Simly who has been the real fuel within my engine. To my lovely children Kevin and Karen for being there for me. All of them gave me the freedom, support, and encouragement to do what I wanted to.

Special thanks to Kiran Somanath for brainstorming with me in the process of building **SOLVE**© over ten years ago.

Brian for being my first partner in the writing adventure. For reviewing and being my sounding board. Also for the real transparent feedback and insights!

The Stimulus team, which stimulates me every day to come to work. For Rakesh who has been my man-Friday whenever required! Rajkumar, Anitha, Jane, Suresh, BK and Mangala for being part of the Stimulus Family. Also, acknowledge Vidya and Aruna for the support and data entry.

Bikramjit Maitra and Rajeev Shroff who agreed to be interviewed. They shared their valuable insights and were quick to volunteer and genuinely support me. Rajeev always had a different paradigm and got me thinking. We even did a late evening interview from the US to support my cause. He's an excellent Transformational Coach & Consultant. Bikram was among the most prompt and supportive Coaches. Thanks, both of you!

To Raam, Ranjitha and the team at Stardom for re-kindling the fire in me to write this book. They also enabled me to do it with ease and grace.

PART ONE:
UNDERSTANDING SOLVE©

BIG IDEA 1 - WE CAN ALL 'HELP' SOMEONE

'Have you got a minute?' It is something we have often heard at work, or even from friends and family. There is someone who needs help or advice to resolve a situation. Especially if you are good at what you do or if you are a key-opinion leader, or if you are a manager, this could happen more often. While resolving problems, most of us are quick to suggest. We later realize that our suggestions do not work for them.

Leaders also give feedback to followers, and we find that the same feedback is repeated year after year. It means that our feedback did not work.

The objective of this book is to have a structured approach to help these people who get such requests. Critical to ensure here that the person being helped owns the solutions, while you stay in control of the situation and ensure they go with clear, doable action plans. For ease of identifying, let us call the leader, aide, consultant or coach as

1

the Helper and the follower or coachee as the 'client.'

SOLVE© is a model which can be used to solve most people and performance issues while professionally maintaining relationships.

This comprehensive model starts with seeking information and ends at evaluating the solution. This model can be used in Consulting, problem resolution, coaching clients and in all modes of helping people. Whether you are a CEO, a line Manager, a functional leader or just an expert at what you do, these five steps will help you help others better.

Lots of 'Helpers' let clients go without finding conclusive solutions while following all the prescribed coaching competencies. Many experienced Helpers and Leaders, on the other hand, are quick to advise. Allow me to introduce you to a universally applicable model which is a recommended approach to guide all 'Helpers.'

SOLVE© *is a model that any Helper can pick-up and use as a thumb-rule for any 1 X 1! You don't need to be certified or credentialed to help others!*

PART TWO: MODEL OVERVIEW

BIG IDEA 2 - SOLVE© A THUMB-RULE FOR COACHING AND CONSULTING

SOLVE© is a model that can be used at home or work. It can be used effectively in coaching, and it can also be used in a consulting situation. Anytime there is a need for one on one problem resolution, **SOLVE**© is a great model. For this reason, I choose to use the term **'Helper,'** which can be inter-operably used to denote a coach or a consultant.

S - Seek
O - Observe & Outcome
L - Listen
V - Value-add
E - Evaluate

Consequences of poor 1 X1s:

- The absence of belief in the institution of Coaching and Consulting
- Poor employee engagement and low commitment to solutions
- Low morale of the followers
- High attrition, loss of good talent
- Your reputation as a key opinion leader is impacted when you are an expert yet, you cannot help others.

Nikhil Sharma ponders on his past experiences as a first-time manager, 27 years ago. I will walk you through that painful memory. He remembered the time when he had an indisciplined team member. His efforts to discipline her completely went awry. He told her things she already knew. He never listened to her perspective. Looking back, he wished he had a more calibrated approach which was more consultative. As a Manager, historically he had been responsible for results and the bottom-line. However, his approach has changed now. Nikhil's experience has taught him many things, and you as a reader can leverage on all of Nikhil's learning over that period. His learnings and techniques are incorporated into an approach called **SOLVE**©. This is an approach for all of us who influence other people and their behavior or performance.

The year was 1992 Nikhil just got promoted as a first-time manager. He wanted to make a good impression on the team that he inherited. He had a team meeting at 0700 am with the morning shift folks. One senior team member Sarah came in only at 0730 am. He was upset and angry! His opening statement to her was 'Sarah, when is your birthday?' When she asked why, he told her that he wanted to buy her an alarm clock for her birthday. He continued to play the role of being her manager. He told her "every day at 7 o'clock if you are alive or dead, I don't care. I want you here at work, and I don't see this as negotiable". He said this in front of the team which was junior to her. Everyone except Nikhil knew that she had an ailing mother at home and she was the only caregiver.

Nikhil did not try to understand what she was going through. He did not let her speak when she came in. He did not listen to her. Never asked her engaging questions. Did not get her to realize the importance of being a role model. He disciplined her in front of her junior colleagues. He closed without any action plan between them. The next day morning, he got Sarah walking in with her resignation letter.

You may all have faced a Sarah or have been in Nikhil's shoe, demonstrating his kind of behavior sometimes in life. SOLVE© is a model which will help in times like these. SOLVE© is a tested and proven model, to aid the leader(helper) during such crucial OR challenging times.

In most businesses, we realize that people are our most significant costs. Results, successes or failures are achieved through people who carry out various tasks. Employee engagement is often a limiting factor. A lot can be accomplished, if, at critical times, we engage our clients and followers in those crucial conversations, helping them to arrive at solutions while getting them to feel valued, respected and motivated to act on the answers.

As I walk you through SOLVE©, I am confident you will appreciate the depth of usable content and the way it is structured. As your mastery in the use of SOLVE© grows, you will find your impact in one on one conversations with people increase proportionately. SOLVE© will be your 'go to' model to reflect and validate your process.

We have seen many approaches to coaching. Traditionally coaching is a non-directive approach. As a credentialed coach and practicing coach for a long time, I realize that approximately 61 percentage people who are being coached prefer a non-directive approach. However, we fail to recognize that 39 percent of the clients need directions. The effort to create insights and active questioning may not be enough to arrive at specific action plans. **SOLVE**© is an approach which blends both the directive and non-directive methodology in coaching and consulting.

Some often asked questions:

Is this a person-centric or a problem-centric approach?

SOLVE© is essentially a person-centric approach. All coaching and guidance are meant to help the person involved. However, **SOLVE**© integrates the need to manage performance as well ensures that we have an action-focused tangible result. So, it balances the two, while it is leaning towards a person-centric approach.

Should we ASK or TELL?

SOLVE© is necessarily an 'Ask' approach. However, there are instances wherein we notice that the 'Ask' is not bearing results, the Helper is within rights to share a story and attempt to create insights. Many orthodox coaches will call this as inappropriate. However, as a manager, there are instances where you need to drive a result and not keep it loose or open. This is yet done after the 'Ask' approach has been tried multiple times. 'Ask' is a better approach. It also helps us build relationships and ensures the ownership is with the client.

As mentioned earlier, this can be used in multiple contexts, which includes coaching, consulting, parenting, guiding and other 1 X 1 approaches.

In **SOLVE**$^{©}$:

- S stands for Seek – Nikhil should have sought information about Sarah by connecting with her before he handled her. As a Manager, we need to know our employees.

- O stands for Observe and Outcome – Nikhil should have let her explain to him what she was going through. He could have handled her privately rather than in front of others. He could have defined the outcome he was looking for from Sarah before he did much else.

- L stands for Listen – Nikhil should have listened to her, let her know that he understands her struggles which she was willing to share openly.

- V stands for Value-add – Nikhil could have created some insights in her mind about the importance of being a role model. He should have concrete action plans so that the behavior is meeting expectations. He could have also created some alternative action plans which were not thought about in the past.

- E stands for Evaluate – Nikhil should have ended with clear next action plans. Plans which can be monitored and followed up, to ensure that the organizational expectations are met, while she is also engaged.

EXPERTS SPEAK (Excerpt from an interview with practitioners):
How do you differentiate Coaching and Consulting?

Bikramjit Maitra:

In my perspective, both Consultant and Coach need to help clients. However, one significant difference is that Consulting is like an advisory role as far as the consultant is concerned. The Consultant could give suggestions and, provide solutions. While in Coaching, Coach needs to help the client to get to the solution on their own.

Rajeev Shroff:

Well, I don't do a whole lot of one-on-one consulting. Most of my work is with organizations. While there are people involved, my focus is more on transforming organizations rather than individuals. I still work with them to transform their thinking, which in-turn collectively transforms the organization. I take on execution projects where I recommend transformation and transform them.

In my opinion, in coaching all answers come from within. While in consulting, most answers come from the consultant. The consultant uses a blend of his own experience, knowledge, and solutions to drive the change. In coaching, rather than offering solutions, I go through a more in-depth process. All answers come from within, and there is no directive work at all, unlike in consulting.

Nikhil's reflection if there was a Sarah again:

> *Seek to understand, then to be understood! Correct in private, praise in public!*

BIG IDEA 3 - SEEK THE DATA, FIND OUT THE STORY BEHIND THE NUMBERS

Preparation and gathering information before any engagement is critical. Without this first step, we've seen many Helpers work in the wrong direction. First impressions are not always right!

Consequences if 'Seek' does not happen appropriately:

- Schedule failure - Inaccurate scope and time is budgeted for the engagement.
- Poor quality leading to client dissatisfaction, reputation of the Helper is at stake. The Helper may not be considered for any assignments in the future.
- Incorrect prognosis - The Helper and client work with incomplete information, often leading to incorrect solutions.
- Time wasted, since the Helper may be proceeding in the wrong direction, and re-work is required.

- Failure of overall engagement - since we are often working on the wrong problem definition. Low client and helper morale. Also, money is wasted.

Case-Study – Seek in Action:

Some years ago, Nikhil decided to help others and moved into a new role as a Consultant and Coach. Some months ago, he got a request from the President of a large organization to coach his direct-report. The President mentioned that his follower - Ram was moving up the ladder from the General Manager's role to a Vice President's role. He wanted Nikhil to Coach and prepare him. He was clear about Ram's requirement and gap areas. He shared the strengths and gap areas with Nikhil the way he saw it. He also mentioned that Ram had to be coached for six months. During the call, Nikhil asked the President if he had competencies defined for the next level he was moving to. Over the call, they both realized, that they required to analyze the needs better and they need to evaluate Ram with the next level of competencies. Since these competencies were yet to be defined, they decided to start there.

- They involved the HR leader, Ram, and people who knew the role well to define the competencies.
- Next, they established and refined the competencies, their definition, description and specific behaviors required within each competency.
- Based on the newly defined competency model, Nikhil designed a 360 Degree survey.
- The survey was completed by stakeholders including bosses, subordinates, customers, and peers.
- Nikhil then got the 360-degree report printed and shared this with Ram and got his perspective on strengths and opportunities.

- They were also able to stack rank the top few competencies and behaviors. Ram also identified the bottom few competencies and behaviors.
- They made a note of things they thought were important. There were also other perceptions they decided to work on, while Ram thought that these might not be real gap areas. Nikhil also realized that Ram had more strengths than were first mentioned by his President. No surprise he was chosen for this role.

The Learning:

Before we connect with any client, get as much information. Ask questions, interview stakeholders, seek data.

Seek is about gathering information before you are involved in any coaching, consulting, advising or helping engagement.

What kind of preparation should you do?

- Preparation would involve asking the individual what he or she wants to achieve before an engagement. This could be possible in some cases.
- Call the person and give him or her an overview of the project. Also ask if he or she has any conditions for the coach, that he should or should not talk about.
  - After building a relationship, first, seek permission to ask questions and contract. Define each other's role and set expectations. If this is a confidential Helping engagement, define the confidentiality and the standard ethics which will be practiced.

- o Define frequency for the meeting, what his perspective is, what his learning expectation is and more.
- o Discuss what is within the scope and what is not. If the client has some specific requirements, respect it and acknowledge the request.
- o An often-forgotten step is for the Helper to sell himself to the Client. Since the client may not know enough about the Helper, would be useful to share the vision and mission of the Helper, with his experience and competence. This helps build credibility in the mind of the client. A lot of this could be done remotely before the first face to face meeting, as part of preparation.

- There are stakeholders which include the boss, peers, colleagues and others who have a perspective which could be unique. Get this if you can.

- Get past reports, recent psychometrics and all available information which the client would like to share.

How does this work in the client interface?

We have all experienced a customer context like a bank or a credit card company. When we call them with a query or a problem, the first task the agent does after verifying the identity of the caller is preparation. He or she pulls up your data and looks at your account, the transactions, the history, and the past call logs. All of this is done before understanding the current reason for your call. This is how it works in a client interface.

How does one do this with employees?

Employees are the most fragile commodity in any organization. It is important that before one engages in a conversation with employees, we need to assess the employee's behavioral strengths and bright spots. It is also important to ask what kind of opportunities and threats does this person come with. Employees are often involved in repeat interactions with us. We realize that if we have a million people, we could have a million people types. There has been a consistent effort to group them into similar patterns. Many Consultants and Coaches see the process of identifying behavioral preferences as a limiting pattern. They argue that we are limiting their potential when we attempt to box them. However, recognizing basic models have been critically useful in my interventions. While many tools exist like MBTI, DiSC, and others, I have chosen to refer to DiSC by William Marston as an easy to use approach. Have chosen DiSC since it is an observable (behavior- based) language and more easier to observe, even for a layperson

We often see some behavioral tendencies.

A. Some of them may be very pushy, problem-centered and like challenges. Marston calls them as the 'Dominance (D)' folks.

B. A second category may be ones who are big picture people. They like interacting with people and are motivated by meeting and being with people. Marston calls them as the 'Influence (I)' folks.

C. The third category of folks are generally in the comfort zone and would like to go with the pace of the environment. They are quick at saying "yes." They may not push back. One of their core values is 'accommodation'. Marston calls them as the 'Steadiness (S)' folks.

D. A fourth category is a group of people who are very analytical. They ask a lot of questions. They like data. They love rules and processes beyond Microsoft Excel or Pages. Marston calls them as the 'Compliance (C)' folks

My learning from DiSC (by William Marston):

It is important that the Helper can assess personality types. As a student of psychology, we realize that in today's world, if there are a million people there may also be a million people types. Good researchers and psychologists have attempted to group them. An example of a good approach is William Marston's work on DiSC. According to Marston D, I, S and C stand for distinct tendencies that we all have. They demonstrate certain specific behavioral patterns or preferences.

- Dominance or 'D' folks are people who thrive on handling problems and challenges.

- 'I' or influence includes people who love to work with people and who thrive on influencing others.

- Steadiness or 'S' includes people who want to go with the pace of the environment. They do not want to rock the boat.

- Compliance or 'C' is also called as conscientious. C's are highly process abiding people. They deliberate and ask a lot of questions. They do a lot of analysis before they arrive at any decision.

If we can understand our client's preferred tendency, then we would be able to treat them the way they want to be treated. We would also be able to support some solutions which are aligned to their preferred personality styles which they would appreciate. If you treated them the way they want to be treated, there is a higher chance that the person may respond amenably. They may also actually apply a lot of the solutions that they commit to.

If we were to evaluate our employees, we could often categorize their preferences into one of the four tendencies listed above. This is also useful when we consult, coach or lead our team members.

This evaluation needs to be done before the first Helping conversation. In addition to these, we may also gather past data and other metrics.

Interestingly, we are not attempting to put people into boxes. We realize that an individual is not only one type. However, we are a combination of the typical four.

All our personalities are a result of conditioning. Our environments shape us. Our parents, friends, teachers, hostels, schools, all contribute to our behavioral patterns.

All of this is often defined as conditioning and shapes individual personality.

Going beyond personality assessments, 360° surveys are also extremely useful in understanding levels and perceptions. Many Coaches and consultants prefer a custom-built 360 before any significant intervention.

All these steps are ingredients of Seek which is about gathering information or preparing before we go in for a Helping conversation.

How does SEEK work in handling poor Employee Engagement scores?

Employee engagement scores often indicate the commitment level of employees to the organization. Employee engagement surveys are designed to bring out the stories of employees. However, most managers increasingly focus on a score. They work hard to improve the numbers. They fail to realize that they need to get the stories and behaviors behind the numbers. Getting these stories to the front and working on these behaviors are part of SEEK. Understanding behaviors help us manage them. We cannot influence and change numbers. We only can change and influence behaviors.

Do clients have clarity about what they want?

Most clients who contact 'Helpers' do not understand the real need. Remember an HR Manager of a large corporate contacting us for a Team building intervention. After analyzing symptoms and asking more questions, we realized that the need was a Leadership intervention. Asking and drawing out these symptoms before we engage in an intervention is also part of SEEK.

EXPERTS SPEAK (Excerpt from an interview with practitioners):

Q1. What kind of preparation do you do before you engage in a Coaching conversation? Could you share a personal story if there is one which is shareable?

Bikramjit Maitra:

It varies from client to client. Let me explain this by sharing my experience with a large organization. We were trying to work with a group one level below the CXO level, with a broad portfolio responsibility of over 1000 Crores. We worked on a Consulting model based on another consulting organization. They would collect demographics and a lot of details about the person to be coached. I also got a summary of the individual's last three years of appraisals. In another situation which was similar, I also did a 1 X 1 with the Coachee's reporting Manager. During that interview, I could collect information about their background, their role, and profile.

Regarding the data collection, I could say it is highly organized in case of MNCs, compared to small companies. MNCs have a well-structured approach and better authenticity in data provided. Often this is around focused 360-degree survey. Different organizations use different psychometric tools A psychometric tool also provide useful data. These data provide a big help in planning the initial phases of coaching.

Rajeev Shroff:

When I started coaching formally, I would spend a fair amount of time going through my previous coaching session notes. Being early in the game I would try to look for insight into the person's mind and trigger or give the information about what he must do differently. My initial coaching sessions tended to be in a corporate style of mentoring, like 'you seem to have a problem in listening and here are three things you have to do.' My understanding of the problem of listening came from previous session notes. In the past, I have said 'I have seen from my notes of analysis of conversation with you about this listening problem. This is how you have to fix the listening problem'.

Now, I have completely moved away from that. I hardly do any prep-work anymore, as I've found that, the more I prepare, the more involved I would be in directive coaching. It causes me to plan, engineer and orchestrate the session. If we plan this is how the session should go, then it is no longer that individual who is driving the outcome of that session. It is pretty much me driving the whole session. We do that in the corporate world as we know that there is already a plan, you execute, you get the person to get things done because they will do what you ask them to do eventually, but the transformation or permanent change you are looking for will not happen in them. I have completely moved away from that, and I now let the person drive what happens in that session.

There is a plan from end to end over the complete assignment, and I run that plan for eight to ten months with the various stages of coaching. Some of these could include data collection, action plans, creating goals so that you ensure the person is moving forward. There is also tracking in mind, to check whether we are making progress from session to session. So, tracking allows you to monitor what's happening between sessions, letting us decide whether it's working. The structure is there, but I no longer drive the path towards the end goal, I let the individual assume control. As an outcome of that, a couple of things happened. Like most of the people I worked with, were considered only if they were interested in transforming. If HR asks me to coach someone and I see no willingness in the coachee to change, I would back off from taking such an assignment.

Most people who are smart who want to take their career ahead or transform, they work well with this structure. I put together the first couple of sessions, and they come up with goals, and they track progress, I don't. Eighty percent of the time, my clients share their status and progress. I get an update from them saying, that was beautiful, or it was a struggle. I no longer drive this. I see that they drive the whole progress.

I find now that more focused I am on preparation and solving the client's issue for them, the less effective I am. I need to have them drive the change.

Q2. Does HR always know what is happening?

Bikramjit Maitra:

My experience is not very good. HR & L&D groups often handle coaching. They operate more as a contracting organization. In most of the scenarios, after they select the Coach and build a plan, they feel their responsibility end. In most of the cases, their knowledge of the client is also very cursory. Never got good help from them. The supervisors were of more significant help. In two situations, they wanted to know every detail of the discussion. I had to put my foot down since this would have meant violation of confidentiality. For instance, I was asked to share about the coachee and what they think about the organization. I disagreed to do so, explaining to them it's unethical and said any details shared would be shared by the coachee. I also went to an extent of saying that "If any further requests are made in this direction, I would like to discontinue as a coach here."

Do you think that they were completely wrong with this request?

I further feel that coachee' s supervisor can do a better job than his HR. It's important to share about the coachee to HR only when you feel the coachee is not of sound mind, or paranoid when dealing with; or he could be a threat to the organization in future if this information about the coachee is not disclosed. Unless such extremes happen, they should get feedback only from the Coachee and not from the Coach.

Rajeev Shroff:

There are multiple layers or levels of this problem. It may start with some reason that can be very hush and coaching is made to be something like an esoteric concept. Coaching happens in a closed room, and it's just left to interpretations, as to what the outcome may be.

Especially with Senior people, HR may not want to step on any toes. They are very careful. In our country I guess, it could be done a lot better. However, in a recent assignment with a global company, there were a series of discussions with HR, even before the coaching started. They were very clear about the process. They were also clear about how they wanted the reporting of progress to happen. They run a very mature executive coaching global program. We had many discussions around how we measure effectiveness. A lot of expectational transparency.

There are pros and cons of this. The pros are that the organization ensures that the investment is productive, and you know results come out well. The disadvantages are that there is too much structure and flexibility for the coach is limited.

The coach selection process is critical and should go beyond 'are you ICF certified or not,' HR should provide clarity on why the intervention is planned. Many times, HR is not connected with business as they are running their agenda.

In the end, measuring returns is very important. When we do not measure ROI, we are doing a disservice to ourselves as coaches. As a practitioner, I have heard "from our experience with coaching, it has not been successful. We didn't see any progress". I often ask 'what progress were you looking for? What were you measuring?' If you do not mention what you were measuring, you may get some sub-optimal results.

SUMMARY:

- Gather all information and relevant metrics
- Understand the story behind the numbers
- Talk to the right people
- Seek information about behaviors observed and gather evidence based on facts
- Seek for permission to contract and clarify what is 'in-scope' and what is 'out of scope.'

A thought that has helped Nikhil:

> *We cannot change numbers, we can only influence behaviors. Get the numbers as part of Seek, however find out behaviors that lead to numbers and then it will look manageable.*

Big Idea 4 - *Observe,* define the *Outcome* and the real need behind the need

One should always start a conversation on a participative mode. It is critical that every Helper starts in a stage of observation where we understand the problem before we prescribe a solution. 'O' also represents the outcome. The Helper needs to at this stage define the outcome or the goal for the conversation.

Consequences – If 'Observe / Outcome' does not happen appropriately:

- The 'Helper may miss some early critical cues.'
- We may prescribe without understanding the issue.
- Very often our thinking can alter the course of our conversation.
- The client may not have confidence in the solutions worked out and may not give you enough credibility.
- To the client, you may come across as being thoughtless or un-empathetic
- You may not register some of the feelings and challenges which the client is experiencing.

Case Study - Observe in Action:

We have all been to a doctor while suffering from an ailment. Remember the time when I had a cold and a cough, went to the doctor we regularly go to. The doctor asked me a lot of questions. Among them were - if I traveled recently; if I had a pain at specific spots etc. The Doctor asked me to open my mouth to make all kinds of noises etc. and then he prescribed some medicines. Spent about 20 minutes with him. On my way out, stopped by at a drugstore to procure the medicines.

At the drug store, they had all the drugs except one. Not motivated to drive anymore, I decided to call my wife and explain to her that I could get all except one drug. After she asked me which drug and I named the drug, she said that we had it at home. I was surprised. Soon as I got home, I discovered a prior prescription with the same drugs. The doctor had prescribed the same drugs he prescribed a year ago, which meant, the doctor knew what to prescribe before I walked in! When I asked a doctor friend why they do this, he explained that all doctors have patterns. He also said that the questions are asked to assess their prognosis and to build confidence in the mind of the patient.

Imagine if you had a doctor who stopped you from explaining and just prescribed. Would you be happy? The doctor was also probably delivering value for the money collected. Unfortunately, we as 'Helpers' seem to prescribe before we understand!

Nikhil's story:

Remember the time when John approached Nikhil with a requirement to help him with his poor time management. John got very critical feedback from his boss and was unable to improve himself despite his best efforts. John was told that he was disorganized in managing time and he had a challenge handling multiple priorities.

Many years ago, Nikhil would've straight away focused on John's planning and prioritization competence. He would've also advocated some best practices he followed. Currently, Nikhil decided to hold back his natural tendency and decided to ask questions to verify his prognosis.

When Nikhil started asking more questions, he realized that John did not have a challenge with managing priorities. This was not even a challenge with managing time. However, there was a more significant challenge with his preferred style. Nikhil realized that beyond time management he was conditioned to a specific pattern. He was used to saying 'yes,' like many Asians. We realize that we are more 'yes' masters and culturally we are unable to say no, even if the situation warrants it. Noticed that Nikhil's client was quick on saying yes, even if he internally disagreed. He would not be able to push back the stakeholder who had an unreasonable demand. This impacted the other tasks he was involved with. As a result, he had this great inability to re-prioritize the other tasks which he was involved in. Often both the old and the new task would suffer. Nikhil realized that often people do not see what they need unless we as 'Helpers' can observe the need behind the need. This can be done through effective probing. Unless we do this, we may not be able to arrive at the right solution.

The learning:

It is important that the Helper stays neutral and let the clients talk. This may also help him assess the preferred personality-style of the client.

'Dumb is smart'

This was an interesting line I heard many years ago. This is especially true in all forms of coaching and consulting. It is known that a Helper should not offer or recommend suggestions or solutions very early in the helping cycle. It is therefore told that dumb is smart.

If you're a Helper or if you're a negotiator, it is essential that you speak lesser and ask more questions. Especially in negotiations, we realize that people who talk more give away more. Therefore, it is told that dumb is smart in negotiations. Classically we find that the person who talks lesser and who does not divulge or open his cards early often gets a better deal, and the other person who is more talkative ends up giving up more. Like a negotiation, a consulting or coaching conversation also holds some similarities. We need to ensure that the client talks more, and the Helper primarily asks a lot of questions.

How does one ask questions?

A great approach to asking questions is to start with the open question. Open questions encourage the client to speak. If the client has a requirement, it's important that one starts with a question which permits the client to speak at length. So, it's important that all of us as Helpers have a list of questions. Primarily open questions in each of our transactions, to begin with.

The probing triangle is a set of questions which could guide you.

- Start with open question(s) to identify the need.
  o Purpose – Understanding the bigger goal and requirement.

- o Sample questions:
  - ▪ What is the desired outcome?
  - ▪ How will you know when you've achieved the goal?
  - ▪ What about this goal is not clear?
  - ▪ What do you think is best?
  - ▪ How do you want it to be?
  - ▪ What are we trying to accomplish?
  - ▪ What does success look like?
  - ▪ How will you know you have achieved this goal?
- Use a closed question to summarise our understanding of the need.
  - o Purpose: Clarify our understanding of the need. Repeat our understanding of the need and ask 'is this really what you want'
  - o Sample question:
    - ▪ My understanding of what you're trying to achieve is...
    - ▪ Tell me if I am right...
    - ▪ Is my understanding right that...?
- Probe to generate options
  - o Purpose: Help the client generate his own options. Ask what options come to mind?
  - o Sample questions:
    - ▪ What are possible solutions?
    - ▪ What are your other options?
    - ▪ What else could you do?
    - ▪ What other angles can you think of?
    - ▪ What have you not yet explored?
    - ▪ What other possibilities are available to you?
    - ▪ What factors should you consider when deciding?
    - ▪ What are other successful folks you've known done in this space?
    - ▪ What are the benefits/downsides of each option?
    - ▪ What if it works out? What would that look like?

- Closed questions to identify the best option
  - **Purpose:** Help client choose the best option
  - Sample questions:
    - Which among these options makes most sense to you?
    - Among all that you have narrated, what seems to be the best option to you?
    - If you were to pick one of the approaches, which would you?
- An attitude question to check if the solution addresses the problem being presented
  - **Purpose** - Check the individual's commitment to the shortlisted option, ask what obstacles may show up.
  - If the attitude question does not bear a positive response, return to the open questions.
  - Sample questions:
    - Are you okay with this solution?
    - What excites you about this? Concerns?
    - How does this decision help you accomplish your goal?
- If the answer is affirmative, ask commitment questions to define next action plans.
  - **Purpose**: Define who will do what and why.
  - Sample questions:
    - What is your action plan? What will you do? When will you do it?
    - How will you know that you've been successful?
    - How will others know that you've done it?
    - What obstacles do you anticipate?
    - What support or resources to you need to get it accomplished?
    - What could stop you from taking action?
    - What do you need from me? When should I follow-up?
- Check if the client is happy and close if 'yes'

The Probing Triangle

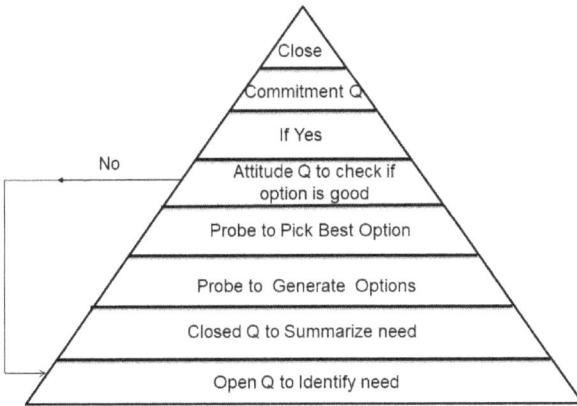

Are there situations where the client lacks ownership?

There are many situations where the client lacks the ownership to fix the issue. Many times the problem was not well defined, and there was a problem behind the problem, which was not uncovered. Sometimes it is because the client was not engaged in generating options. Many Helpers prescribe very early in the interaction, and the ownership or the monkey is on the Helpers back, and it has not moved to the client's back. So, it's important that the Helper asks questions and gets solutions from the client so that the ownership for the solutions generated are with the client.

Application to parenting: Nikhil narrated an incident. He remembered the time when he came back after a journey and found his wife instructing his son. She continually repeated her expectations of their son. She spoke, and the youngster just heard her out. May sound familiar to most parents. In this case, this was about the quantum of time he was putting into studies. Seeing Nikhil, his wife said 'Nikhil – why don't you speak to your son. I am tired of telling him'. Nikhil's first realization was that any more telling would bear no fruit. He wanted to keep her happy too. Nikhil agreed to speak to their son, under a condition that his wife would be present along with him. Another condition was that she should not speak or contribute when he was dialoguing with the youngster.

After getting her buy-in, Nikhil started asking him a few questions about his studies and how he was doing. He mentioned that he was doing okay and would pass in all subjects. Nikhil continued to ask him if just passing was enough. He asked him how the best students in his class were working. He also asked him if his two hours a day which included homework was enough for him to score well and secure admission into a good professional course. After a lot more questions, his son agreed to do more. Nikhil asked how much more, and they negotiated a deal for him to study two more hours, in addition to what he was doing.

The question - 'how was Nikhil's approach different from his wife's?' She was telling, while Nikhil was asking! **SOLVE**© is a lot about asking. Asking also helps generate ownership and buy-in in the client's mind, since the solutions come from the youngster. There is a higher chance of application, compared to the 'tell' approach attempted by Nikhil's wife.

Why ask all these questions when we already know the solution?

Returning to the doctor's example, it's a fact that when patients come to a doctor, the doctor knows up-front what the problem is and what the individual must do. However, if the doctor straight away prescribes, then the patient loses trust in the doctor and that prescription. So, it is important that we can follow the doctor's approach. If you noticed, what the doctor does is, he asks a lot of questions. His questions may include – 'how did it start? How long since you've had this challenge? Can you describe it? Can you show me where exactly the pain is? etc.'. After doing all this, the doctor seriously considers the data collected. A little while later he may give you a prescription and you see a lot of value in that prescription. This is because the Doctor made every effort to understand your requirement.

How is asking questions linked to the value we deliver?

When a doctor asks a lot of questions, we get the feeling that the doctor is attempting to understand the real problem that we have. The questions are linked to the value we perceive. We need to make a difference in each client's life and contribute to his bigger **'why.'** The client has a big purpose. Are we as 'Helpers' able to deliver a solution and answer the bigger why? The more valued 'Helpers' who are higher paid are deemed to deliver more value. The money we bill as 'Helpers' (Coaches and Consultants) has a big relationship to the perceived value we offer our clients.

How important is establishing the outcome in a Coaching or Consulting conversation?

When you observe and can understand the client's context, the real output is that the outcome is well defined. The Helper asks for specific outcomes and pins it down to the critical few. The Helper could also assess how the outcome could be measured. Assessing and focusing on metrics used will help quantify the change later. The Helper tries to help the client visualize the image of success. He also checks for motivation. A sample question could be: 'How would it feel, when you reach your goal?' While closing the interaction, the Helper again re-affirms the commitments and could check if the client considers the solution as Manageable – The Helper could ask the client to clarify their commitment – 'what are you committing for this goal?'

What is the result of the '*Observe / Outcome*' phase?

The outcome of this phase is the definition of the problem or the outcome. As is often told, 'in the definition of the problem lies the solution.' When this outcome is well set and defined, sometimes we're already arriving at the solution without going through the rest. The Probing Triangle is a quick short-cut to get to the solution, without going through the other steps of **SOLVE**©. Very often the individual states one goal and means another.

So if you're following this approach, then you'll be able to understand a lot more before you prescribe. This is the essence of Observe.

EXPERTS SPEAK (Excerpt from an interview with practitioners):

Q1. How important is understanding the personality before you coach or consult? Could you share a personal story if there is one which is shareable?

Bikramjit Maitra:

I have used different Psychometric tools, and MBTI is one of my favorites. I could share my personal experience of coaching with one of my clients, young, academically brilliant from the US. His MBTI report showed him to be an ESTJ, with E & J being very high. He claimed that he was the youngest Vice President of a globally famous large Organization before taking up the current role. He began by saying 'Bikram, I don't think you are the right person to Coach me.' When he was reminded that the organization already made this choice, he decided to continue this call.

MBTI was a great starting point for me to offer him help to understand himself. He was a high achiever, with a chip on his shoulder.

As I presumed this coachee would ask for data, I prepared the same and arrived at my insights based on reports generated. I asked whether the coachee faced issues during meetings, where he gave his viewpoints too strongly and too quickly. He readily agreed and added "Yes I do face it often. When I find people beat around the bush, I always like to cut through the crap. But maybe because of that nobody agrees to my point, although I am right". We discussed that we could not change the world, but we could change the way we do things. We looked at things he could do to change and help his situation in a very neutral mode.

During the next session, he confided that his wife was very appreciative of the session he had with me and she saw herself as the biggest beneficiary. I realized that he was eloquent with his speech, short-tempered and quick. The psychometric analysis cued me in these directions.

Rajeev Shroff:

Interestingly I find that its more relevant in consulting than in coaching, which is probably the reverse of what people would say. I never do any psychometric testing at all, I'm dead against it, but it is very useful when it comes to consulting. Let me give you an example.

I was working with a global company on a consulting assignment. It seemed like their business was being eaten up by start-ups and companies deploying artificial intelligence. This business was getting commoditized. I saw that the problem to a large extent was the CEO himself. He had preconceived notions about what would or would not work. I had a choice, I could either go in asking him to fix things, or I could get into his mind, understand and help him realize what they were doing wrong. Given the person's strong personality, if I battled with him and told him 'Mr. X, what you are doing is wrong, this is what you need to do', I would not succeed, and the whole purpose of the project would go to waste. I went back and changed the entire conversation, to ask several probing questions. Once he started answering these questions, he understood what the issue was. Post that when we discussed solutions, he was a lot more agreeable.

As far as coaching is concerned, I feel anybody should be able to achieve almost anything they want to achieve and realize their full potential. They are only limited by their thought process, not necessarily defined by which of the 16 profiles they are from. I see that enough times. Each time it convinces me more that the only limitation is in their mind regarding what they want to get to and do what they want to do. Say someone wants to be a CEO of the company, run their enterprise, it's up to them. Why do we want to put them into a box, and decide as the reason why they are not good at marketing? I cannot see the value in that approach. By 'boxing' we are limiting the Coachee's possibility to 1/16th of the individual's potential. It doesn't make sense.

Even when you look at the 360-degree report, the data points can sometimes be limiting because it is the view of the rest of the world on what the person should be doing or shouldn't be doing. As long as it's used to show the clients some direction, and build self-awareness, these tools are useful.

Q2. Are all clients clear about their goals when they come to you? Have you had a situation you can share, where the need behind the need was very different (from the first need expressed)?

Bikramjit Maitra:

An experience I could share was related to coaching a senior person from the US. When I studied his background, I realized that his background is very very different than most I have coached or worked with professionally. I found that he was just equivalent to 10th grade as far as academics were concerned. He ran away from family and found work in the construction industry.

Later, his father requested him to join him in his small hardware and software company, where he had some customized product to sell, mainly telecom based. He was the CEO of the company until his company was taken over by the large company which engaged me. I was the coach there. After taking over, the CEO of the company had become an employee of the larger company. His role was more functional, comparing his general role with his previous company.

Also, Mr. X started by volunteering his personal story of the last 18 months in great detail. It seemed that he had a lot of difficulties in his personal life. He lost his father, and he had sold shares of the company along with his sister to support their mother. Meanwhile, he had to go through a second marriage and became a father. He said when his need for money was the most, he lost all his savings in the form of stocks he had.

The one hour scheduled session went past an hour. I allowed him to vent and listened to him completely without interrupting him. When he realized that he had taken much more time than allocated, he apologized profusely. But later I realized that the session had helped a lot to build a tremendous amount of rapport.

The need expressed by the organization was to make him functional. However, I realized, that the need was much more than to make him functional. It was more important for him to realize that he was no more a CEO. Employees from his bought-out company were no more his responsibility even though they continue to work with him in the new company. He also required to balance both professional and personal life and need to be more functional, undergoing training and mentoring for his current job in sales.

I could build a good rapport with Mr. X. We together got to the real problem beyond his originally expressed issue. As mentioned earlier he also insisted that I hear about his past, personal life. This helped me steer the conversation into the professional life and got working on some good action plans. This was an example where the need behind the need was very different.

Rajeev Shroff:

Clients often share whatever is at the top of their head. We usually get three sets of answers. The first set of response comes from HR as the originator, 'I think their delegation skills are poor.' At the next level, an increasing number of global supervisors would say 'lack of business skills,' and the person being coached would have heard all the buzzwords – influencing skills, executive presence, and so on. We must peel the onion to get to what would help transform the individual.

A Digital media company recently promoted someone internally as a COO. This individual used to manage sales and marketing earlier. The person came and said he wanted to understand how to manage 'the operational rigor.' He now had various functions he never used to run earlier. He never did weekly or monthly reviews etc. Someday he wanted to become the CEO of the company.

The coaching conversation started with things like – 'I struggle with dealing with people since my communication skill is not great.' During his 360, all his team members mentioned that he was excellent in dealing with. If he could crack every deal with demanding customers, how he could do that if he does not have excellent communication skills?

So, we went one level deeper only to find out that he was originally from some rural town, moved to a large City when he was in the 10th grade. His classmates bullied him as his English was terrible. It got stuck in his head that he was not good enough. My work was half done, once we unraveled that it was just an issue of confidence.

Q3. How do you typically start a coaching conversation?

Bikramjit Maitra:

Initially, it would be a casual conversation with non-controversial topics. This is followed by an introduction between each other for around 20 mts. The idea is to put the coachee at ease without discussing much of coach's credentials, (as sometimes coachee is already aware of the coach's profile).

Also, I give more importance to the language of coachee, which he can speak more fluently or more comfortable with, where he could be more expressive. I call this language capability. This helped me easily analyze the character or have a proper understanding of him and his goals. Sometimes I also share my vulnerabilities, e.g., I am working on my listening skills, etc.

For instance, my first client, who was academically brilliant and required more of figures and statistics may speak more vibrantly than the client who too was very senior yet did not have a good command over the English language but fluent in Hindi. While I was not too fluent in Hindi, initiated to speak in Hindi in-between, to get better communication with the Coachee.

Rajeev Shroff:

So, this is the whole process end-to-end.

The first phase: I collect as much data as I can for a couple of sessions, including 360 degrees feedback, I go deeper in their mind, and help them surface where they want to go.

The second phase: Form goals, strategies, and help them decide how to get there, what is the leverage they want to achieve.

The third phase: Execution, and tracking progress.

The process changes to an extent when I work with people who are going to be with me for only 3-4 sessions. In those situations, I am very mindful about the investment in time and money they are making, so I start getting deep in the first session itself.

I ask them what problem they are facing and what they wanted to get resolved. The story behind the story is sometimes skipped in the process. It is risky, but they get what they wanted. It works well, where a person wants to change, they have a problem and are focusing on getting results.

For senior leaders where they want to see the substantial transformation, rather than problem-solving, then the first 1-2 sessions may include two to three hours of just getting deeper into their minds.

Q4. Do you have a sequence of asking questions in your coaching practice?

Bikramjit Maitra:

If I have a summary or background of the coachee, then my questions will be about it. I summarize my understanding and seek his comments.

Also, if I have a report of any psychometric tool or analysis, say the 360-degree report, my talk will be based on that as a starting point. I follow a model for identifying a few areas of strength & improvement for each Coachee. I want to focus more on the strengths. Take a specific example of cricketer Sachin Tendulkar. He focused on batting rather than bowling while practicing. Extending that example, I think we need to focus on strengths more in leadership development.

So, focus on the area of strength and find the areas of improvements surrounding it to make it better. Also, discuss with him or her the opportunity areas and allow the coachee to choose the areas he or she would like to work on. I sometimes give them a format to list their areas and from there identify the two or three areas we need to work on.

Rajeev Shroff:

There is a logical sequence for sure. I would start with an overall generic question 'What would you want to work on today'? Alternatively, 'what you are dealing with?' People often ramble off four-five areas they want solved.

I would track these four-five things in my mind. I would then take each one of them individually and ask follow-up questions and do a complete deep dive. While I choose not to arrive at solutions for each area at that point, I move on to the second and the third point. After I cover the depth and the width of the areas or issues, I see that solutions start to emerge.

Sometimes by deep diving, (beyond creating insights), you find that there is a pattern. We can identify the more significant issues and, we realize in this process that some of the points were trivial and are not consequential. This helps us focus on the bigger blocks. If we don't dive deep, we may miss some real issues.

SUMMARY:

Step 2: Observe and ask for the outcome

- Dumb is smart. Reduce the talk as a helper.
- Establish the Outcome
  - Ask for Specific outcome – pin it down
  - Ask for Measure – how will you measure?
  - Check for Motivation –, How would it feel, when you reach your goal?
  - Check if it is Manageable – ask the client to clarify their commitment – what are you committing to this goal?
  - Observe behaviors and evaluate the personality type (optional)

An ideal sequence of questions:

- Questions about the Current Situation
- Identifying impact and consequences
- Unpacking the underlying need
- Use the probing triangle. Move from open questions to Closed questions

Nikhil's reflection:

Often what the client initially seeks, is not what he really needs. Ask questions, get to the need behind the need. Define the real outcomes. Dumb is smart.

BIG IDEA 5 – BE A REFLECTIVE LISTENER

Listening is an important skill for any Helper. Half the Helper's role, half of all conflict resolution, influencing, leadership, a large part of problem resolution is often an essence of good listening skills.

Consequences of poor listening:

• Erosion of trust – Trust is the foundation of most helping relationships. If you are a doctor, a lawyer, a leader, consultant or a coach our clients first trust us and then choose to approach us. Poor listening is the single largest reason why most 'Helpers' are not approached. If they sense that you jump to conclusions based on superficial details, they also conclude that you don't care enough about them. While building trust takes time, it leads to great benefits as a Helper.

• You stop learning – The most enriching part of a Helpers role is that you continuously learn. You learn through other's circumstances, and we all get emotionally and intellectually developed. Poor listening leads to poor learning and limits your growth as a professional.

• Impatience is shown to your followers - The ability to be a good listener takes time, and you need to develop it with regular efforts over time. However, as you gradually get better and better at listening, an automatic benefit is that you develop patience.

• You will have lesser clients if you seem unapproachable. As you present yourself as a patient listener, people feel more naturally inclined to consult with you.

• Wasted time and money – Many clients who approach 'Helpers' who are poor listeners leave with the feeling that they wasted their time and money.

• You may not detect and solve the real problem - As a helper, you should always be attentive to what clients have to say. Especially if you are a leader or manager, listening to clients will help you understand what needs to be changed and you could then work towards retaining talent and making improvements.

Case Study - Listening in Action:

Nikhil's current organization conducts Training programs in addition to Coaching and Consulting interventions. Remember the time a few days ago when one of his large customers asked Nikhil's Business Development Executive for a proposal on Leadership training.

Her approach:

• She understood the focus audience as leaders.
• She made a note, and she asked questions which were related to her understanding and her direction of thought.
• She captured the needs, she justified her feelings

through her questions and sent out a proposal for leadership training.

The real need though was a "Train the Trainer" program and the need from the client was for Nikhil's team to teach the senior leaders how to conduct a "Train the Trainer" program. If this was understood well first, then the proposal would have been focused. If the proposal were to address the real need, Nikhil's organization would have got that business at the first shot. We need to understand that a lot of business is lost due to poor understanding, resulting from poor listening skills. A lot of customers have just one repeated challenge. They say that 'this person doesn't understand my need.' We hear this between partners, husbands and wives and otherwise in a lot of relationships. The often-used phrase is 'You just don't understand me.'

The Learning:

Listening is an important part of any relationship. If one were to listen effectively, then most conflicts and issues could be eased out, and we only have situations. Not problems. For a helper, it is critical that one understands the struggle, the problem at the root cause. Not what is just shared by the client, but more importantly what is the problem behind the problem. It is important to get to the source of the issue after evaluating the real challenge, and that can only be done through good listening skills.

Look at two people in conflict. 'You call me a word, I call you a word!'. There is so much talk and quick challenging. Very little listening happens. If you were to listen completely to a disagreeing party and think win-win, then often the conflict is diffused.

The advantages of good listening in coaching and consulting conversations include:

- helps you demonstrate you are listening
- encourages clients to share thoughts and feelings
- prevents misunderstandings
- allows them to feel understood

Reflective Listening

Reflective listening is the ability to focus completely on what the client is saying and feeling about the situation at hand. It is also the ability to understand what is important to the client and to support the client to talk about his or her concerns, thoughts and desires. It involves showing to the other person that you have truly understood the essence of what the other person is attempting to communicate and the emotion behind the intent.

Under the pretext of listening, we find a lot of people who fake listening. We hear people who say, "yes go on," "I am with you." We all do this to some extent. Many others blatantly demonstrate disinterest and poor listening. Mobile phones and laptops today are major distractors when we're at 1 X 1s. Shows the other person that we're not completely there for them. We are also disrupted when we speak to a loved one or at a place of worship or a meeting of any sort.

Once I heard a senior gentleman comment 'these days people have the money to buy a phone, but not the wisdom to use it!'

We need to stay completely focused on the 'here and now.' Listen to what the client or your follower is attempting to say. Observe the words, the unsaid emotions, observe the body language and tonality. There is a lot more of the message there. Anger, frustration, joy, surprise, etc. are either explicitly expressed or implicitly indicated. Be there for the client, as part of that conversation completely and continuously. Listen to the said and the unsaid. That is the ask from reflective listening and the expectation from each Helper.

Reflective listening is demonstrated when we summarize the key essence of our understanding back to the speaker. An additional component could be if the emotions are also picked up and reflected. A golden rule often used suggests 'if you hear a paragraph, you give back a sentence; if you hear a sentence, then you give back a word.' Essentially what you reflect should be shorter than what the speaker spoke about. This shows to the other person that you have truly understood the essence of what the other person was attempting to say. More important than the words are the feelings that are demonstrated and read by the listener. So, if I were to be very frustrated and angry and upset with something and if I shared a problem with you as the listener then not only would you summarize and say 'what I hear you say is, that you have a struggle handling the dysfunctional behavior of Shiva, especially his loose comments.' You may like to continue your sentence and say,'… and I see why you are frustrated with this, and I see why you're angry. From your point of view that sounds completely justified'.

How does one use it?

We could use it in regular conversations; at interviews; client meetings; at coaching conversation and most other situations. You have an opportunity after you have heard out a problem statement from someone, after someone has spoken for a long patch or even when an instructor speaks or shares something on a one on one conversation. All of these are instances for you to reflect the fundamental essence of your understanding to the speaker.

Key idea:

- Focus when listening and eliminate distractions
- Attend to verbal and non-verbal cues as well as the words that are spoken
- Inquire to draw out the client's ideas

Common issues in reflective listening

Some of the common issues that people demonstrate during conversations include being distracted by various thoughts. They are involved in other things. Especially as Asians, we tend to be involved in multiple tasks at the same time. One of the researchers called this polychronic behavior. A polychronic system is one where several things can be done at once. We seem to be involved in many thoughts. While it does have strength in multi-tasking, to the client, it indicates a lack of interest and focus.

- We edit the listeners' narration to suit our context. The client information, as a result, gets distorted.
- The biggest concern is we are not able to focus on the speaker in the 'here and now.' We seem to be disturbed visually with a lot of distractions.
- Sometimes it's the mobile, other times it could be a laptop, other times it could be a piece of paper. Our eye contact often is not towards the speaker.
- One of the other big struggles noticed which impedes effective listening, is the urge to interrupt.

Know someone who I know very closely who says, "If I do not ask this question now, I will forget it later!" If we are faced with this challenge, why don't we use an effective method of writing down some of those questions that are coming to mind? Why don't we have a pre-defined part on a part of a notebook where we may write questions that come to mind and hold back the interruption until the speaker completes? Therefore, the second big piece is an interruption.

Another one that one can think of is that we are not able to completely focus on long sentences for a prolonged period and then we tend to zone out. A great approach is to say 'Aha! Okay, I understand', Occasionally we could repeat some of the keywords spoken by the client. This would be critical to show that you are completely with that person. Maintaining eye contact, visually not being distracted, holding back your questions are some best practices for good listening.

How much listening is appropriate in SOLVE©?

SOLVE© is a model which is very listening centric. If you need to solve client problems and fix issues, we need to stay with at least 75% of listening and asking questions. The Helper speaks up to a maximum of 25%. The rest is done by the client. The 25% of Helper's contribution will include asking questions, sharing stories and paraphrasing. We do not want to be suggestive. Some of the researches state that this percentage could go as high as 90 percent of just listening and asking questions.

It is important that we can summarize conversations, our issues and problems the way we read it. Take permission and challenge the client, all these are important roles played by the 'Helper.' It is important that the Helper asks very pertinent questions and remain in the here and now.

Do all personality types like it when we listen to them?

- Largely speaking "Yes." Most people like it when we listen to them. We sometimes find people who demonstrate a high 'dominance' behavior. They love it when we listen to them. They also feel respected and are unconsciously influenced when we demonstrate good listening. These are the ones who are focused on problems and challenges. They like to speak their mind out, and they expect others to listen to them.

- This also applies to the people-centric person who would love to influence others. They may not be the best at listening. We also know they are the ones who fake listening. However, they still like it when others listen to them. They love it when others are appreciative of their ideas which are very often out of the box.

- The third category includes people who want to go with the pace of the environment. DiSC studies of William Marston call them as the 'Steadiness' folks. They often would like to go with the pace of the environment. They are good listeners, who rarely speak. They may have ideas, but rarely present their ideas to a larger team. We need to ask them more questions. Preferably open questions. It's important to get them to speak, and it is important to show that they have a voice at the table. Therefore, listening to them and demonstrating active listening is something that they completely appreciate. These people don't often speak up even if they have an idea or thought. However when they speak, they want to be listened to.

- The last category often noticed are the compliance-oriented or the conscientious folks according to research types by the William Marston in DISC. These are the ones who are very analytical in their thinking process. They have a lot of data, they are not quick to speak they are often the last ones to speak, but when they speak, they want to be heard and understood. They wanted to make sure that you have understood their data in depth, which is often well researched out.

- All personality types like others to listen to them. Who wouldn't? Ask for the most common issue between a husband and wife or two partners and the biggest struggle mentioned is 'he doesn't understand me, or she doesn't understand me.' A lot of that understanding starts and falls in place with effective listening.

Have we noticed people in conflict listen to each other?

Listening is critical in conflict management. When we look at two individuals who are in conflict, what is commonly seen is - 'You call me a word, I call you a word.' When people are emotionally raging, they make statements and are quick to rebut before the speaker completes. As an example, if you and I converse with each other and if I were to ask you 'what are you passionate about in life?' While you respond, imagine I don't even listen to you. I rubbish what you are coming up with, and I enforce my idea. We notice before you complete your sentence, I am saying something else. If we were to do this to each other, we notice that we are going to end up in a conflict. Also, most conflicts follow this pattern. A pattern where both individuals are not listening to each other nor let others complete their sentences.

Take a completely different situation in the same context, where you make a point, and I listen to you completely. I also ask you relevant and supportive questions. You notice me make a genuine effort to understand your point of view. After I have understood your point of view if I was to summarize and say so here is what I hear you say, and I hope I got that right. Then if I was to ask you "I see your point of view. I also see why you are saying what you are saying. However, as a different option with no force to follow it, what do you think about this...?" If I was to think win-win, listened to you completely and then proposed an approach which was genuinely win-win, do you see this conflict resolving?

Listening, therefore, is a very important part of all conflict management. Staying in reflective listening defuses a lot of the conflicts and removes conflicts from happening in the first place.

In Coaching and Consulting situations, the ultimate objective of good listening is to establish the current situation. It is also meant to understand the 'said' and the 'unsaid.' This involves a lot of asking questions and reflective listening, working in tandem. Ask questions to unravel the client's challenges. You may even ask a scaling question – on a scale of 10, where are you right now? After the complete understanding is achieved, we are in a better position to value-add and create insights for solutions and action planning.

EXPERTS SPEAK (Excerpt from an interview with practitioners):

Q1. Is there a best practice you can share on listening skills?

Bikramjit Maitra:

One of the things I do is I encourage the coachee to speak at length. However, this may vary in certain situations. If the coachee is a talkative person or overtly extrovert, you can hear him speaking continuously or listen with patience till you interrupt him with the next question. When you get a chance, summarize your understanding so far. While an introvert needs to be pushed by showcasing your failure or opportunity areas, which again blends with authenticity and humility. This helps him to open little more.

Rajeev Shroff:

Initially, when I was starting with my journey, my mind would be working on finding solutions.

My mind would be working on:

- What is the next question I should ask this guy? or
- What would be the most interesting question? or
- He should feel that I have asked him a smart question? or
- How do I solve this issue?

It is tough to not focus on our performance. It takes a while to let that go and realize that this is about the other person. The pressure to outsmart the other person must go. Even the next question should come from what the coachee said and not from your intelligence at all. This is a hard one to let go. Our job is to listen and observe the visual body cues and to listen entirely. Mastering this takes time.

In the corporate world, I would not be listening since I already know the answer. I would have gone prepared and give very little time to the other person to explore options. There is no listening. From that state to being a Coach is a massive transformation.

How did you hold back from this urge to active questioning?

Many of us do wear multiple hats, coaching, training, consulting and so on.

I can switch contexts, as a fractional CEO, I am running an organization, there is no way that I will not ensure progress to happen, I make sure all things go smoothly, which needs a lot of effort. If it's the customer, you are working for then you must work with the context of your customer and not with yourself. Many of us work with the backdrop of ourselves. What we want to achieve is the least relevant part. The moment you can push your ego out of the game, you can switch context easily.

 Not being perceptive about the other person will be the biggest disservice you can do to yourself. In the coaching journey, this part is tough to do. The other thing is that nobody is watching you as you are in this relationship with the individual. There is so much temptation to think you will make faster progress by just giving all answers. I learned all this the hard way that there are no short-cuts.

SUMMARY:

Step 3: Listen to the said and the unsaid

- LISTEN TO REFLECT the content and feelings behind what they are saying and check for understanding
- Stay in the present, be completely there.
- Ask more open questions and reflectively listen
- Establish the current situation (Ask & Listen)
    o Ask a scaling question – on a scale of 10, where are you right now?
    o What are the challenges here?
- Observe and reflect the emotions beyond the words.
- Stay with the context of the client. Do not edit client information.

During 1 X1s, remember the golden rule for reflection:

When you hear a paragraph, you reflect a sentence; if you hear a sentence you reflect a word.

SUNIL GEORGE

BIG IDEA 6 – WHEN YOU VALUE-ADD, CREATE INSIGHTS, GET THE CLIENT TO THINK NEW SOLUTIONS

Value-add includes discussing the challenge, goal, problem or the situation and seeking options. It involves creating insights in the client's mind so that the person can do new things and think in new directions which the person had not thought of so far. This step aims to exceed the client's expectation by thinking about those new solutions or new directions. Before the client approaching the Helper, the client may not have thought about this new direction. However, after the conversation, the individual sees this as a great new way.

Consequences – If 'Value-add' does not happen appropriately:

- The client thinks about the obvious few choices he earlier considered. The Helper did not create any new insights.
- We end up in 1X1 conversation that is not providing value.
- When the client or sponsor (often the client's supervisor who has initiated this intervention) sees

no value, the reputation of the Helper is at stake.

- Clients when they leave the discussion, feel cheated and are internally dis-satisfied.
- Loss of repeat clientele for the Helper.

Case Study - Value-add in Action:

Often it is easy for Helpers to explore options and ask questions to have the client generate options easily. Remember a time when Nikhil was conducting a 1 X 1 conversation with Raina. He was helping her maintain a record of the learning events and track her progress. Nikhil was attempting to generate options from Raina. He wanted the solution from his client, as was suggested in his 'Coach training session.' However, he found himself at the end of the road, when Raina started saying 'I don't know' for each of his questions. Every time Nikhil asked a question about how she would do something she said, 'I don't know.' This pattern repeated, and she refused to look at the possibility. Nikhil still wanted to get the solution from the client.

Nikhil remembered a technique he learned. He asked her if she knew others who did well in the area that she struggled. She said yes. The discussion steered into how that successful person operated and what he/she did. She came in with some options which were very insightful. They discussed if she could have done that herself. They shifted the perspective and got a lot of choices on the table. Value-add is getting this shift in perspective. It's sometimes about sharing a story and creating associations between the story and the client's dilemma, which at the outset was not related. The Helper asks those questions so that associations are built, and action plans are generated. That's the essence of value-add.

The Learning:

We believe that the client has the potential to do more and they have the solution within them. The task for the Helper is to ask those questions so that the Helper can unlock the client's hidden potential and draw out those thoughts from the background and co-create their solutions. That is the essence of value-add. It involves creating insights which the person could convert into action plans. Those insights happen only when the Helper asked those relevant questions.

The coach harvests insights. Beyond analysis, this requires an impartial investigation that goes beyond surface level inspection. Ensure the data is put in context against business issues that matter.

Determine recommendations based on the needs of the client. Check if the recommendations mesh with the client's long-term strategy or short-term goals.

Is there a best practice in creating a Value-add?

Value-add comes in combination with us understanding the background and the behavioral preference of the individual whom one is helping. A best practice here is to understand their personality and treat them the way they want to be treated.

What is the platinum rule of relationship management?

We have all studied this 'golden principle' when we were in school. The 'golden principle' said 'Do unto others the way you would like them to do to you.' You were the benchmark. The Golden Rule is something that most of us studied in school, and we took as gospel. Remember getting my first credit card. The person who sold it to me offered me a 'Gold

Credit Card.' He said that this was the best cards could ever get. So, I picked up the most valued card many years ago. At this point, this was the best it could get.

Some years later, banks came in with another card this time called a platinum card. The platinum card was better than the gold card. This to the banker meant continuous improvement and change. Similarly, there's also a need for us to have a 'platinum rule' instead of the 'golden rule' or the golden principle. So here is the platinum principle. It suggests 'treat them the way they want to be treated.' It doesn't matter, what is your comfort or what is your personality. What is more important is to gauge what is the personality of your client and treat them the way they prefer to be treated. This is not about limiting their potential or putting them into a box. This is only about influencing them appropriately.

If the client takes longer, is it okay to give the client time to find his solutions at his leisure?

In coaching and consulting techniques, it is recommended that the Helper should not push the client into a solution. Having said that in today's business world this is far from being idealistic. Every client who pays for a coaching conversation wants to see results. Coaching models which recommended that it is okay to stay with a client and not to push him/ her towards a solution, very often leave the client with a feeling of being short-changed. Consulting assignments, on the other hand, requires clear solutions. So, in the utility of **SOLVE**$^{©}$, it is critical that we can arrive at clear next action plans at the end of each conversation. It is not okay to let the client lose to find his solution at leisure.

How do we know the solution is comprehensive and workable?

We know the solution is comprehensive and workable

when we can apply the solution, and we can see results. A great way to assess this is by asking the client if he or she thinks that the application of the solution would in his or her mind, bring about the solution. It is also useful to discuss where else have we seen this work; in what context have we seen this work and what those actions were.

How does the Helper contribute?

The Helper contributes in a couple of ways in the process of value-add. A unique way the Helper does this is, he/ she asks questions and share his or her own stories where required. Often the story may be an irrelevant incident or a question from a completely unrelated space. Once the client responds, the Helper asks the client to derive some learning from the response or story and glean some insights and convert those into action plans.

The skill is to derive insights that answer necessary client questions. The challenge as always is to know what questions to ask and unlock the hidden insights.

The Helper can talk about situations which are at the outset unrelated. The Helper could talk about a real situation which happened. Then ask the client to understand or to draw out what is the connection that the client could make from that given situation to the individual's solution. We come with a strong belief that anything is connectable to anything. Often, we share a piece of current news and glean from it unrelated learning related to the client's goal. This is best if it is also related to the client's coaching goal at a deeper level. The next question is often addressed to the client - 'what messages do you take from there towards the problem statement we are discussing today?' If the connection is strong, the client quickly generates a very insightful and empowered action plan.

Example: Imagine if your story included two kinds of shoppers in a supermarket. One who came prepared with a shopping list and another who worked with memory. Chances are the one without a list more often shopped for unnecessary stuff and picked up a lot of stuff that the person did not originally intend to. Also, the shopper may have missed some essential stuff. On the contrary, we have all seen that shopper who came in with a prepared list, went straight to the right sections check marked on the list and went to the next section for the next item on the list. Imagine I ask my client (who does not have a recorded learning plan and does not make linked progress) –

- What did you notice there and what kind of insights can we draw from that situation into your situation?
- Do you relate to either of the shoppers here?
- What specific behaviors can we adopt from here?
- What insights do you take from here?
- Which of the first shopper's behavior do you do?
- Do you want to change any of them?

Additional Questions:

- What are the possible solutions?
- What are your other options?
- What else could you do?
- What other angles can you think of?
- What have you not yet explored?
- What other possibilities are available to you?
- What are the benefits/downsides of each option?
- What factors should you consider when deciding?
- What if it works out? What would that look like?

We often find the client say 'yes, maybe I also can make a note I also can tick off and maybe I need to go back periodically and assess my learning, provided I'm able to capture it.' While this may be a very generic situation, it enables the client to draw connections or associations which do not exist. The strength of the Helper is to narrate these situations and bring it from the background to the foreground and have the client derive those connections.

The coach can share such metaphoric parallels. This will encourage the client to draw those insights. Those insights should lead to some specific action plans. Another approach for the coach is to tell great stories. Often the Helper has had a lot of exposure in the direction of what the client wants to resolve. Sharing stories which are not directly solutions but actual happenings in the world is a key skill. The Helper could protect any client names or sensitive information. The skill of value-add is about addressing the core issue and 'story showing' if the person can show the story to the client, then the client will be able to understand the story and actively draw out insights.

Most of our cultures have conditioned us to study from stories, epics, and parables. This is a great approach. The Helper should be a storyteller of successful cases where things have worked and then step back and ask the client 'what do you take from there?' In a business context, I remember telling a senior client leader in a consulting conversation, that this solution worked there and got them awesome results, however, your context may be different. My client quickly corrected me and started drawing similarities. My learning was that if we could create insights by sharing stories and get them thinking, we could get them to build relevant action plans too.

Have had umpteen situations where the client has a specific problem. I step back, and I talk about a story which probably is an incident in my life or maybe another situation that I have heard someone face. I narrate the situation and talk about the story. I talk about the content, and I talk about probably some of those action plans that the client took away from that situation. Then I will step back and ask 'what do you take from this case?'. Do you see any relevance here? Hopefully, the client would be able to come in with some solutions or insights which are beyond which was anticipated or thought of at the beginning of the conversation.

The coach also needs to check for completeness. Which means the coach needs to assess if these solutions or insights that we have worked out will solve the problem at hand. Checking the confidence level of the individual in applying that fix is also an important step here to check for completeness. Beyond what the Helper thinks, what matters most is what the client thinks.

Creating Insights Using Stories

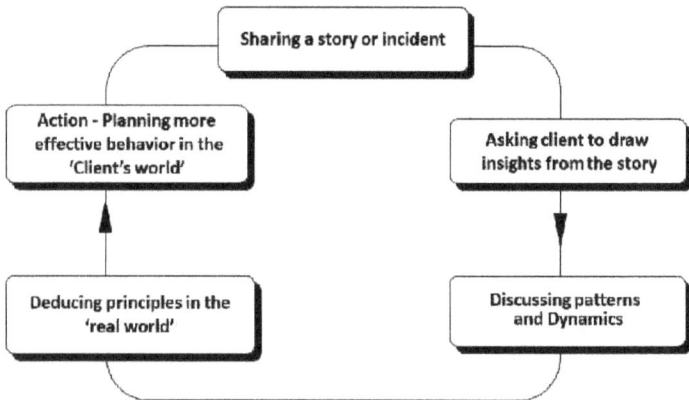

Going beyond stories, we could use:
- A real incident
- An interesting piece of statistical information
- News articles

- Metaphoric pictures – E.g.: 'Points of You' cards
- Quotations

Should we check for motivation and confidence to apply the solution?

The coach should always ask questions which could later come up in the client's mind. For example, I often find that when the client tries to apply the fix in his or her world the client finds a struggle. The client finds real-world problems, and challenges. Motivational issues and other people's negative thoughts often rub off on the client. This results in the client not applying the action plan.

The coach's role here is to ask those difficult questions which will enable the client to think about the possible obstacles or roadblocks that could come up in advance, in the real world. Once the client attempts to apply some of these solutions, I would ask questions like:

- 'What struggles do you see or could come up when you try to apply this fix?
- In another case, I often ask 'Let me play the devil's advocate and let us say that this one condition that you laid out is not there. Then what would you do?'
- Let us assume that your boss does not behave this way that you expect him to. What would you do?

These are obstacles which the coach needs to forsee and ask the client for what he/ she would do in that context. The objective of asking these questions is to encourage this person to see those roadblocks well in advance. The coach should check for motivation and the confidence to apply any solution.

Could the Helper suggest a solution as a last resort?

It is recommended that the Helper does not recommend a solution, while it is important that the client is going out with definitive action plans. That poses us a million-dollar question - 'what should the helper do here?'. It is important that the helper asks questions and share stories which can create insights in that person's mind. It's perfectly okay to give the client an assignment to work on, but there must be a definitive next action plan. In a worst-case situation, it is okay and within the reasonable right, for the Helper to provide feedback. However, this needs to be laid out as 'consider.' This needs to be shared as feedback. We would like all 'Helpers' to also master the skill of direct communication where required. We would like 'Helpers' to be honest, appropriate, respectful and direct in interventions that we are involved in. This is truer as a consultant, where solutions may go quicker to the client. The Coach may still do this as a sparing last resort. From Lore Consulting study, it was found that 39% of clients preferred a solution from the Coach. (Source: Bacon, Terry R. 2004. Effective Coaching, Fourth Ed. Durango, CO: Lore International Institute, 2004). So, it is okay to do this as a last resort.

Position the direct communication as feedback. When giving feedback, use the four-step process:

1. State the antecedent which is the standard or behavior expected.
   - E.g., On time delivery is critical for any project

2. Share observed behavior or the absence of it. E.g., This is what I saw you do, and this is what I hear you say; this is what I noticed.
   - E.g., You mentioned that three of your four projects are behind schedule. You also said that this was

due to scope creep as per your perspective.

3. The impact or consequence to the person or business.

- E.g., As a result, the overall time to market of the bigger product may be impacted, especially when three of the sub-projects are behind time-lines.

4. Afterward, ask the action plan question. Get the action plan from the client.

- E.g.: 'So, the question is what would you do to prevent this from recurring?'

We're hoping that the client could come in with some of his action plans. If the coach was to state, that 'this was expected, this is what you did and here was the consequence; step back and ask what you could do as an action plan? With that, we're hoping that the client can come in with an action plan.

If the client doesn't, then I believe as a Consultant or a Leader, your role enables you to say, 'would you like to consider this as a choice?'. Classically, leaders and consultants have this flexibility, while many 'Coaches' may not have this flexibility. The coach could yet suggest or offer a 'consider' note after everything else was tried. However, it is important that a coach or even any Helper does not impose or tell. The best option is to use great questions so that the clients can arrive at their solutions.

A suggested sequence of questions to create insights and deliver Value-add:

- Questions to understand the context
  o What happened?
  o When does this occur?

o What's going on?
o What else?

- Questions to check motivation:
  o What do you see for yourself in the long term?
  o What is most important to you? and/or
  o How is that important to you?
  o What led you to make that decision? and/or
  o What were the factors in your decision?
  o How do you feel about that?
  o How confident are you? and/or "What obstacles are there?

- Questions to check impact:
  o What would happen if X occurred?
  o If you do (or don't do) this, what could happen?
  o What would be the impact of X?
  o What's the worst thing that could happen?
  o What's the best thing that could happen if you engage the new behavior?
  o What is the consequence of X?

- Questions to deep dive or expand options:
  o Can you tell me more about that?
  o Given the gap, what specifically can help you?
  o What options can you think of? Or what options do we have here?

- Questions to evaluate options
  o Given the outcome planned, let us shine some light on each of the options.
  o What is appealing about this option?
  o What will indicate success?
  o What evidences will tell you the option is

working?
- Questions to blue print the achievement strategy
  - o What actions do you intend to take now?
  - o What are your action plans?
  - o What do you intend to Start/Continue/Stop doing?
  - o What resources are required now?
  - o What support is required?

EXPERTS SPEAK (Excerpt from an interview with practitioners):

Q1. How do you create insights in the client's mind? Could you share a personal story if there is one which is shareable?

Bikramjit Maitra:

If you could share your personal experience or story, it becomes one of the options for the coachee to consider. I try to share something like Coachee's problem with what I did or seen people do, rather than give a solution.

Let me explain this by providing an example.

A person say Mr. Y, good with his technical skills refused to share his expertise with others in the organization as per his boss. If he could have shared, the organization could have been a great beneficiary. Both Mr. Y and his peer were handling a big business belonging to one client with two different divisions. Mr. Y is handling the bigger chunk of the business and rest is handled by his peer.

Where I had a coaching session with Mr. Y, during the process, I asked him, "Why don't you exchange each other's knowledge?" (with his peer). He answered saying as their jobs are different, it does not make any sense. After thinking about it, he came back in the next session and said that the bottleneck was that there was no forum to share.

I challenged Mr. Y to create a forum and call a meeting, and He was worried that his peer would refuse to participate. I still held on to the same question what stops you from calling a meeting as Mr. Y handles a major chunk of the business. Mr. Y responded, "What if he refuses?" I further challenged him, and he went ahead and scheduled a meeting.

Meetings were held and luckily in their third meeting client was invited to be present, and they were able to sell a huge project.

In my fourth session with the coachee, I was given a gift (a pen which had been gifted to Mr. Y by his client). Mr. Y placed a small chit which said, "You made me call that meeting, and all the success is due to you" When we probe and challenge, insights happen.

Rajeev Shroff:

I think for me the most significant way to create insight is silence. Sometimes I would get to a point where the person feels that he has explored whatever he could explore and at that point, it is easy and tempting to suggest. Many of us are tempted to say 'have you tried this? Would you mind trying this way?' etc.

Sometimes the person would say 'I know you are forcing me to think of the answers, but I am stuck.' At that point if you could hold back and if their mind is still churning, all you must do is give them more time. It's hard. A minute of silence will be a lot of time. Most often with that approach, some breakthrough does happen. Some new insight will come if you say, 'what else,' 'what else have you tried' and will get them to shift their plane. Also asking how a leader or well-wisher they admire would do in the same circumstance etc. will be very useful. A lot of time silence helps because you don't need to shift panes. You just need to go deeper.

SUMMARY:

Step 4: Value-add when you work solutions

- Create insights, get the client to think about new solutions
- Establish Options / Solutions (Ask & Listen).
- Look for role models – ask what they would do in this context?
- The Platinum rule of relationship management - Treat them the way they want to be treated.
- To create insights beyond using powerful questions, use stories; a real incident; an interesting piece of statistical information; a news article; metaphoric pictures and quotations
- Remember to give feedback which is specific and non-judgmental
- Use the ABC (antecedent, behavior, and consequence) approach to share feedback

Nikhil's action plan:

> *Ask powerful questions, so that you unlock the client's hidden potential and draw out those insights. Help them think their own solutions, which were not in their radar earlier.*

BIG IDEA 7 – ENSURE YOU EVALUATE. WHAT YOU INSPECT, THEY RESPECT

Evaluate includes two parts — the definition of clear action plans and follow-up after implementation.

Consequences – If Evaluate does not happen appropriately:

- Action plans discussed are superficial, and real application remains missing.
- Money is wasted.
- Client and Helper are unclear about next action plans
- No change in the real world. If there were action plans, they are soon forgotten.

Case- Study: Evaluate - E in SOLVE©

Nikhil had umpteen situations where he had given feedback or reviewed a team member, and after a period he noticed that there was no change. He remembered a time many years ago when one of his direct reports Jeff who had been working with him for a long time was being reviewed for the past year. He discussed the year that was, and he looked at Jeff's performance against the objectives set. He reviewed Jeff's actual strengths, his opportunities vis-a-vis the goals that were set. On Jeff's opportunity areas he discussed different approaches. He continued conversation into other areas. He closed the conversation, shook hands and parted. Nikhil continued to observe Jeff since he was his Manager. A month, a quarter and a half year went by, with no change.

Nikhil approached his Mentor Coach for guidance. After they spent time together, Nikhil realized that he had not closed that conversation effectively, clearly defining the next action plans. This stage of defining next action plans is this part of 'Evaluate.' It doesn't stop there though. It continues into the leader following up with the individual later to see what the actual application and change has been.

The element of confirmation before we close a conversation and the element of follow-up together is what is called as ''Evaluate' in this model 'SOLVE$^{©}$.'

Nikhil's critical misses – the critical parts of an Action Plan

When Nikhil closed the conversation and defined action plans, his action plans should have comprised of the three minimal components - 'who', 'what' and 'when.' Simply put, 'Who' will do 'What and by 'When' are the three critical components of this summary.

- Who - Nikhil needs to define the actor or the doer of the action plan. He should not leave that loose. Is the follower Jeff going to do something? Is Nikhil expected to provide any support? Whose action is it?
- What - What specifically is the action to be done? This should not be left to the imagination. We need to define what will be done as the verbal action.
- When - The third component is 'by when? Nikhil

needs to have timelines which are clearly defined and realistic.

Nikhil could have clarified the action plans of Jeff, the support (if any) Jeff expected, and specific timelines for each of the actions. These become the components of an effective action plan.

To re-affirm the actions decided and to confirm execution possibility, Nikhil decided to ask:

- **When do you intend to start?** – This was an effort to specify the start date.
- **What checks and measures will be in place?** - This was a question to control self-defeating behaviors.
- **Who will help you review your progress Vs. plan?** Is there someone whom you want to contract with? – Nikhil saw a need for self-monitoring or someone who Jeff could use to monitor and give him some feedback.

Should we document action plans? Who is the owner?

Action plans need to be documented while this could be documented by Jeff or by Nikhil, ideally both. While either or both could document the outcome, the responsibility of the follow up belongs to Nikhil. This is all the truer since Jeff is Nikhil's team member. When he performs, Nikhil also benefits. The ownership for follow up rests with the Helper. Orthodox coaches may disagree with this approach. However in today's business context, we owe this to the sponsor who expects change and ROI. The orthodox approach leaves a big efficacy gap.

Should we set reminders and who should do it?

Nikhil later learned an efficient approach for setting reminders. At the end of a coaching or a consulting conversation, he would send in the minutes of that conversation. He would send this mail which would summarise and list the biggest bright spots; the challenges; the areas discussed during the recent conversation and next action plans.

The summary could include:

- Date and schedule of the conversation
- If this is an ongoing discussion, then a review of the past action plans:
    - o The Bright Spots
    - o The Opportunities
- The goal or topic which was discussed during the current conversation
- Next action plan – with 'who, what and when'
- Follow-up or next meeting date and plan.

The template used by Nikhil:

ONGOING SUMMARY TEMPLATE

Client:	Coach:	Date: Time:
Status of Action plans:		
What is working:	**Challenges:**	
Area discussed during the recent 1 x 1 Session:		
Next Action Plans:	**Next Follow-up Schedule:** **Date:**	

One of the best practices Nikhil used is, he would mail the summary to the client and mark a copy to himself. When Nikhil got a copy of that mail, he would drag it and drop it into the follow-up date on his calendar. On the follow-up date, he would get a popup reminder on his calendar, which indicated that he should be following up with this Client. He would forward that mail to the Client and request for a status update. This enabled his client to think that he was following up and passionately cared for his client. In critical conversations, Nikhil decided to take ownership of the outcome, and this is how he used technology to follow up.

What happens after the conversation?

After the conversation, the Helper Nikhil was advised to be mindful and watch-full of actual change which is happening in the premise with the client. Nikhil decided to be observant. After checking contractual obligations and seeking explicit permission from the client, Nikhil decided to wear his 'Manager' hat and sought feedback from the client's peers and others identified by the client. However, this need to happen after explicit permission is sought or as agreed during the coaching contract.

Jeff (the team member) on his part decided to document his action plans in a place where it was easily discoverable. Jeff considered it a best practice to go back periodically and evaluate himself against those action plans so that he is reminded to follow up on those commitments. These are the actions which Jeff and Nikhil decided to do after the conversation.

What is the importance of follow-up? What happens if we don't?

For all of us parents who have kids, we may have experienced this situation. We ask a small child maybe a four-year-old or a five-year-old child to brush his or her teeth before the child goes to sleep. Imagine a situation where you tell a child to brush his or her teeth, and you never bothered to check. We notice that the child in his or her mind thinks that parents had to say this now, so my parents also did it. After a certain period, the behavior backslides, and the child forgets to brush his / her teeth at night. If you cared for your child's teeth, you probably call the child and ask "hey did you brush your teeth? Come here. Show me". If we do not follow up, the child goes back to the original practice or behavior. What we inspect, they respect. Likewise, in Helping it is important that we can inspect so that they stay committed to their action plans. If we do not do this follow up, then the client or the follower may slip back into the original state.

Do you recommend any technology tools for follow-up?

Nikhil in his experience used Outlook and OneNote most often. It is a great practice to take notes while we are coaching or consulting. More relevant if you are on a one to one with your team member or business client. Critical to note that it's important that we establish good eye contact. Nikhil developed a useful practice to take permission from the client. He would ask 'Hey I hope you don't mind if I could take some notes. Subject to the client permitting this, the coach could capture notes. It is important that the coach maintains eye contact for the larger part of the conversation.

One of the biggest bugs in Nikhil's past was that he always had a laptop or an iPad or in front of him. He has excessively focused on gadgets around him, and the client got little attention. His Mentor-Coach told him that this impeded his coaching presence and his listening skills. This often left a poor impression in the mind of the Client. Nikhil would often say 'go on, and I'm with you. Please continue, etc.' However in the eyes of the client, Nikhil was not completely in that conversation, and this did not provide a good impression to the client. Nikhil's Mentor advised him to use a laptop only if required. Nikhil decided to take notes briefly. Just the words maybe or some of the keywords. Nikhil started to seek permission and take advantage of a complete pause in the conversation and then key in some notes. This also enabled his client and himself to absorb the conversation so far and capture some key discussion points before they were lost. Nikhil often used Outlook as a tool to send this to the client later. He decided to send the minutes of the conversation and the follow-up points to each client as a best practice. All the tools and documents used in a coaching conversation were grouped using OneNote so that all related parts were available together.

The debate of ownership - pros and cons of following up in the Coaching profession:

There is a lot of debate within the Coaching profession, as to who should follow-up between the Coach and Coachee. Traditionally it has been thought that the coach should take responsibility for follow-up. This is certainly true if the Coach is the supervisor of the coachee.

Pros of this are, that the Coach has control and is answerable to the organization about the effectiveness of the Coaching intervention. This is today a million-dollar question. Cons of this approach are that the Coach's bandwidth is limited, and the client seems to think that the coach would send reminders, action plan and minutes. This approach shifts the ownership and accountability to the coach, which does not seem right. The Coach should rightfully transfer the ownership, responsibility, and accountability to the client. However, in practice, we see that junior and mid-managers backslide on their commitments. The more committed Managers (often noticed among senior leaders) take responsibility for their action plans. The effectiveness of the Coaching intervention is today in question.

The new approach from Stimulus Consulting (P) Ltd uses a 'Learning Diary' - having a shared tool where the Coach and Client have visibility of action plans, while the ownership is clearly with the client. Visit www.stimulusconsulting.com for more.

The new approach we have used within my organization is a shared tool that the coach and client have visibility. With the debate around 'should we follow up or should the coach not follow up,' we required to find out a midway option. The responsibility for updating the action plans and status updates is shifted to the client, while the Coach has visibility. The new tool we designed at Stimulus is called the 'Stimulus Learning diary.' This tool was custom built to solve this dilemma. Our process within the tool:

- Before a coaching discussion happens, the admin at Stimulus Consulting creates an event(with a specific schedule), and a welcome mail is automatically generated. The Coachee needs to create a login.
- After the coaching conversation is completed, the client automatically gets an email with a link from the system.
- The client is asked to go online and update his action plans. The client goes into a template, and he is asked to input his Action Plans.
- Besides, he can also set a reminder date for follow-up. The system follows-up based on the date set.
- Pre-set reminders are also set at 30 days, 60 days and 90 days which is modifiable by the admin.
- The system also has forms/tools which document progress and stumbling blocks.
- Another automated link generated after 60 days asks the client to share specific examples of application and list stumbling blocks.
- The work-flow permits this form to go to the client's supervisor if the client desires. If the client desires, he can also share access with the organizational sponsor.

The entire process is automated. The coach has visibility to the records and can initiate tools and generate reports for the Organizational Supervisor at a high level, without citing any specifics of action plans. This initiative by Stimulus to use technology has been successfully used over the last few years across numerous interventions. All freelance Coaches must evaluate tools that measure impact and track progress.

Role of feedback in follow-up:

This step of 'Evaluate' enabled Nikhil to see the Action-Plan being applied and tangible change began to happen in Jeff's case. Nikhil also decided to appreciate positive change when he noticed it. He decided to be specific to the feedback he gave Jeff. In the past, Nikhil was used to giving feedback which was vague and judgmental. His often-used words were "You need to demonstrate more passion"; "Your presentation lacked the punch"; "From the heart you're a nice person etc." Nikhil transitioned to using observed behaviors. He started citing actions Jeff did or did not do against expectations set. He got more specific while giving feedback.

Nikhil decided to:

- Be generous with his praise.
- Create a frequency log of the feedback he gave. He realized that he had to catch them doing things right. He decided to give his clients at least three motivational feedback points and only then give one developmental feedback.
- Give employees a positive feeling about their abilities and their work, and he saw performance improve.
- Make a list of the key behaviors that were observed.
- When he said "Thanks," he referred to these behaviors and traits.
- Look for and reward progress, not just the big accomplishments.
- Recognize 'failure' and risk. He called it one of the building blocks of innovation and creativity.
- Recognize the desired behavior or achievement as soon as possible after it occurs.

Ensuring motivation to apply action

Nikhil decided to evaluate the outcome of these actions and check the motivation level of Jeff to apply these actions in the 'Love to be state'. He started asking questions like:

- Moving forward, what excites you about the outcome of these actions? – This question enabled a lot of positive motivation in the mind of the client to apply the action plans.
- How important is this achievement for you? – This question increased the stake in the mind of the client to change.
- What might derail you from your actions? How might you sustain your enthusiasm & energy? – These questions helped uncover positive derailments proactively and discuss action plans. This helped prevent back-sliding of action plans.
- What self-defeating behaviors might you encounter? – This enabled Nikhil to help his client introspect and share derailing behaviors they may demonstrate, which were within their control. This also helped the positive control of those elements.

The effective use of 'Evaluate' ensures that the time utilized is time well spent and is causing an insight leading to change.

EXPERTS SPEAK (Excerpt from an interview with practitioners):

Q1. Do all action plans of clients get applied? Is there a best practice you can share from your exposure?

Bikramjit Maitra:

It depends on individuals with whom you are dealing. Most of the people who give commitments fail to do the follow-up. Following up with them through reminders like calls and emails could help to a certain extent. However, eventually, the commitment lies with them. Most of them tend to go back in their old ways while some of them follow their commitment when they see a good result or get good feedback.

One of the questions I tend to ask each coachee is "How you want to be remembered by the four constituents viz Employees, Clients, Family, Friends & Society"? This has seen to create deeper commitments. All of them explicitly commit to coming back and sharing even after the assignment was over. Yet many a times you don't know if this will happen.

Rajeev Shroff:

The people who are running corporate goals, running operations are very comfortable with their structures, SMART goals and a lot of that. The higher you get, the more disciplined they are. If you are working with Director level person, by the 4th session, they will come back with their actions, plans, measure, etc.

In other situations, I often start the conversation with 'These are the three goals we are working on, which one would you like to discuss today?" That reminds them about where we are, and where do we need to go. What also helps to track is mid-check reviews with the supervisor.

In my practice what did not work was me monitoring their actions. When I did that, I became the owner, and I switched to their supervisory role, and we no longer know how much of the progress is forced and how much is real. It's like me tracking my daughter, by asking her 'have you finished preparing for the interview?'.

Moreover, that becomes my problem than hers. This approach does not work with coaching too. This often happens due to some simple issues – maybe this was an organizational tick in the box coaching assignment.

Are you tempted to take ownership and responsibility for the follow-up?

Of course, I am. However, I know from my experience as you know that those are not going to be our most successful coaching assignments. The question sometimes being asked by HR is "can you take ownership of making sure that person is changing?" That is no longer a coaching assignment.

Q2. Is there any recommendation on follow-ups? Whose responsibility is it - Coaches or Clients? What about in Consulting? Does this change?

Bikramjit Maitra:

Follow-up in my mind is the Coach's responsibility. The initial coaching contract could also articulate this.

As an example, Gary Kirsten (the cricket coach) quit. He used to throw the ball at Sachin(past Indian Skipper). There was a big discussion around who could throw as many balls now. Throwing the ball is the Coach's responsibility, but the players decide how many they will face. Like-wise asking questions, getting the Coachee to think and define an action plan, ensuring commitment, etc. is the Coach's responsibility. But how much coachee will implement and work on, is his / her responsibility. There is only so much one can do for another person.

Rajeev Shroff:

I am sensing the need of shared space of tracking which keeps people honest. As a coach, I see that all assignments should have a place where you could track progress. If you create that space, you can track progress. When the person takes ownership, things happen. A shared tool will help. I am exploring options of these kinds.

How does it change when it is Consulting?

At consulting, I am responsible for the project end to end. So, I do everything including follow-up and ensuring things happen.

What percentage of action plans get applied by the Clients in your perspective?

Rajeev Shroff

Most coaching assignments I do has three goals. For eight-nine months, I do a closing 360, and I ask specific questions on the three goals on a scale of 1-10. Funny to note, that often there is enormous progress on two out of the three goals and the third one may happen only partially. In the grand scheme of things, it would be that one thing which they need to do more than anything else, which would make all the difference.

I don't track actions so much, but I do track transformation.

Some people do not make progress. I can think of a few examples. There was a CEO who did not want to make so much of a transformation. He wanted to use me as a sounding board and sometimes in problem resolution. My approach was to steer it back to him, to ask him 'how would he do it?', so each session became a unique session, by itself. I don't get too much comfort from that approach. However, the basic still says 'do what the Coachee wants and not what you want.'

Anything I did not ask, (which you think will be useful for readers) which you'd like to share?

Bikramjit Maitra

If the client is mature then he may require little effort. It is important to keep coaching results realistic. There is a notion that "anybody can do anything if they put their mind, body and soul in." We need to understand that everyone has limitations.

Capability gets channelized with age and experience. The coach can help fill the gap between his or her capability and what one has actually utilized. One can build a new capability, however the potential is still prone to limitations and may not be infinite.

SUMMARY:

Step 5: Evaluate the actions:

- Confirm action plan – Ascertain who, what, when.
- Document action plans and set reminders.
- Executing the Actions
    - o   Ask, when do you intend to start?
    - o   What checks and measures will be in place?
    - o   Who will help you review your progress Vs. plan?
    - o   Is there someone whom you want to contract with?
- Follow-up is the Helper's responsibility. Use technology to do this. If you're stuck, Try out the Stimulus Learning Diary from Stimulus Consulting at www.stimulusconsulting.com
- Ask these questions to prevent back-sliding – What motivates you?
    - o Moving forward, what excites you about the outcome of these actions?
    - o How important is this achievement for you?
    - o What might derail you from your actions? How might you sustain your enthusiasm & energy?
    - o What self-defeating behaviors might you encounter?

Nikhil had the following insight (beyond creating clear action plans):

> *Traditionally, follow-up has always been the Coach's responsibility. What you inspect, they respect. Use technology to do this. Use a shared tool where the Coach and Client have visibility*

PART THREE: APPLICATION AND TIPS

BIG IDEA 8 - SOLVE© IN COACHING – MEASURE AND MONITOR CHANGE

For most leaders, developing others is part of their role. If you are a manager, then your follower's performance adds to your performance. Many individuals who are subject matter experts are entrusted with the task of coaching others. Few are credentialed and certified to coach. For all these folks, **SOLVE**© is a great Coaching model which provides the basics to   Coach. It acts as a thumb-rule, to practice professional Coaching.

Consequences of poor Coaching:

- Managers today are too busy to coach. They often don't know how to coach.
- Those that do coach usually do it poorly; with little structure, vision or purpose.
- Untrained 'Coaches' 'Tell' more than 'Ask.' They do not engage clients in building their solutions. The clients feel disengaged at the end of the process.

- The ownership of the solution is often not on the client's shoulder.

- Good listening is not a common virtue. Most leaders are high on Telling and poor listeners unless they are trained.

- People often backslide after great 1 X 1s.

- Managers are using coaching to raise poor performance to acceptable levels rather than as a positive management intervention. There is a clear lack of pre-defined objectives and a focus to elevate performance.

- Bad advice from an inexperienced and unqualified coach can take a business down the wrong path, lose significant revenue and growth. Also wastes a lot of time. Ultimately, this will stop the business from achieving its goals.

- 'Coaches' believe that in pure Coaching, we have all the time to solution and let the client go for multiple sessions without defining the problem or moving forward with a solution. This is real money wasted!

Case - Study: Nikhil's evolution and step-wise application of SOLVE© in Coaching

In the past, Nikhil had a difficult time Coaching. He was an expert Advisor. He conducted many 1 X 1s as part of his leadership role, but most were not to his satisfaction. In many cases, the action plans did not stick. People backslid to the previous state though Nikhil had done his best. People were unhappy with his solutions as he was a poor listener. Poor performance affected him and his organization. He thought that they were all bad hires or bad people and he was right with his approach. After all, he told each one of them what exactly he wanted them to do. He was surprised that things were not getting better.

When Nikhil changed his role into a full-time Consultant, Coach and Facilitator, he now had to work with multiple clients and organizations. He did not have authority as he did in the past. He noticed that the skills he learned as a senior leader were not enough in the new role. He decided to get himself certified as a credentialed Coach. When he went through coaching credentialing, he realized that there were different models and approaches which were existing. Every master coach who was involved in the certification process came in with his process. He found some good processes but none of those processes went deep into the analysis which needs to happen before a coaching conversation, and none of them covered the importance of follow-up as it is required in the current context. During his Mentor-Coaching phase, he was introduced to **SOLVE**©. He found it easy to pick the steps from here and use these as the foundation steps in any coaching conversation. This would become a template which he could use as a thumb rule in every coaching conversation.

Today after many successful projects as a Coach and Consultant, Nikhil remembered the time when he was asked for a training intervention by a client. The client asked him for a leadership intervention. They wanted a straight-forward Training program. They did not want a coaching intervention at the outset. However, he realized the utility of Coaching in that intervention.

His logic:

- The group comprised of very senior leaders with distinct challenges which were not common to the group.
- They had been through multiple training programs and had the knowledge to do it all. However, they were not doing any of these effectively, and the organization, consequently, had a struggle. In

Nikhil's analysis, they had a knowing-doing gap.

- Nikhil managed to convince the stakeholders that training wasn't the right intervention. He decided to use a coaching approach with these senior leaders.

- He started with a 360-degree survey to assess the current environment and did an unpack of that 360 as his first conversation with them **(S)**.

- He called them all into a room and showed them how to read the report. He explained the common objectives of the program. He also explained how the Coaching contract would work and articulated the responsibilities of the client and Coach **(S)**.

- He got participants to review their 360 report; come prepared with their perceived strengths; opportunities and specific goals for the project, which was for one year **(S)**.

- In the first 1 X 1 conversation, he repeated the procedure he would follow. He also sought permission to Coach, thanked them and summarized the ethics and confidentiality involved. He continued to coach them to build a laundry list of strengths and opportunity areas **(S)**.

- In the coaching contract very often, Nikhil would discuss the confidentiality clause in greater depth.

- Nikhil's initial effort would always be to understand the background before he started resolving any solution or before he used the rest of the SOLVE$^©$ approach. This was 'Seek' - gathering all the information.

- He decided to work on specific areas each time he coached his clients **(O)**.

- Every session he started with questions regarding their past action plans. He reviewed the status of those action plans and then only got into the day's agenda**(O)**.

- When he reviewed the status of the past action plans one of his questions would always be about what difficulty the client had in applying some of the solutions which they wanted to. He also actively looked for behavioral evidence of application in the client's field of work **(O)**.

- After gathering this evidence, he would discuss the bottlenecks that they have faced or obstacles if any. Only after this, he would discuss the day's coaching goal **(O)**.

- Nikhil would start with asking about the goal. Then he would start with establishing the real problem at hand. Nikhil realized that while the requirement list and overall goals were defined earlier, there may have been some change in context and environment of the client. The client may even have a new perspective on the problem at hand. Nikhil would start by establishing goals for this coaching conversation. He would also ask what some of those pointers or behaviors were which led to this goal. He would ask 'how will you know when this goal is achieved? How will you measure it?' etc. To evaluate their commitment, he would also ask 'what are you committing for this goal?' 'What is at stake? etc. **(O)**'.

- Then his effort would be to observe what the client had to say about the situation and the problem at hand **(O)**.

- His initial effort was to ask an open question and let the individual talk. Having had repeat interactions with the client, he was able to assess already what are these individual's personal preferences and tendencies. Once he was able to assess the problem at hand, then he re-confirmed the goal for this coaching conversation. Nikhil would sometimes ask a scaling question – on a scale of 10, where are you right now? 'He also asked questions regarding why the goal was important and the relevance of having it. After he asked open questions, he moved from the 'Observe and Outcome' phase to the 'Listen' phase.

- His effort was to ask open questions and let the client speak. He asked questions regarding the client's context the client's behavior in the real situation. He attempted to find out how this person behaved. He also made efforts to ask relevant questions. He stayed in the moment and was focused without being distracted. He took notes. He asked questions to draw out the situation. He was also actively involved in reflective listening **(L)**.

- Once he was able to ascertain the situation, he was also able to demonstrate to the client that he actively listened to the client. He did this by summarising his understanding of the challenge. He not only summarised the challenge briefly and accurately, but he also picked up the emotions that his client was demonstrating and empathized with the client's emotions **(L)**.

- As part of Value-Add, Nikhil started asking questions which could create insights in the client's mind. His effort was to apply appreciative coaching. Nikhil stayed positive. He often asked the client "Do you know anyone who does this part well? What do they do differently from you? What can we learn from them?" His effort was to always draw answers to the client's challenges from the client **(V)**.

  o He asked clients "how do we go forward from here? What is the solution to the challenge in your opinion? etc.". If the client did not come up with a solution, then his effort was to ask "did you always have this struggle, or were there times when this part worked well for you? How did you operate then, what did you do? What are the behaviors which we can draw and apply from that context into our current context? Sometimes he would ask – 'What would your role model suggest you here?' **(V)**.

- Nikhil attempted to draw out best practices and solutions which the client saw as valuable and a good option. Only after he created some of those insights, he would move into the action planning phase **(V)**.

- Nikhil came across a few situations when the client repeatedly threw up his hands and said "I don't know" for each of Nikhil's questions. When he saw that the client was stuck, Nikhil decided to share a relevant story from his experience. Then he repeated the question and asked the client if he had any insights from the story. Nikhil's effort was often to share a story, sometimes an unrelated story and ask the client to derive connections and associations from this situation**(V)**.

- Once the client derived those connections, Nikhil would attempt to list the insights the client received. From each of these insights, Nikhil then would ask the client for action plans. Some additional questions included **(V)**:
  o Given the outcome planned, let us shine some light on each of the options.
  o What is appealing about this option?
  o What will indicate success?
  o What evidences will tell you the option is working?
  o What actions do you intend to take now?
  o What are your action plans?
  o What do you intend to Start/Continue/Stop doing?
  o What resources are required now?
  o What support is required?

- Value-add in practice: Value-add intends to push the client to a newer solution and newer directions which the client did not think about so far **(V)**.

- After the Value-add part in the coaching conversation, Nikhil's next effort would be to confirm which of these solutions is the client going to apply. So, he often would ask the client to summarize the choices that he had at hand, and which does he see as sensible or most appropriate. After the client picked up his solution, Nikhil would try to ask how the person will apply those actions. 'What will he do? Who will do it? By when would he do it?' He had specifics worked out from this action plan. After the specifics are worked, out he would attempt to ascertain the client's motivation to apply some of those action plans. So, he would ask questions which encourage the client's motivation to apply and listen to evidence of motivation **(E)**.

- Often Nikhil would also ask what bottlenecks the client fore-saw in the application, which would come in the way **(E)**.

- He did this so that the thoughts which the client could face are pre-empted. All of these are part of the Evaluate phase during the coaching conversation.

- Towards the end of coaching conversation Nikhil always asked the client to send him a summary of the action plans. In other cases, Nikhil drafted a summary of the discussions for his records and sent the client a copy of his notes **(E)**.

- During some conversations, he also asked the client if he considered it ok to send him a status update periodically. In some cases, Nikhil co-created a rhythm (Eg: like twice a month may be on the 15th and the 30th of each month). He expected the client to mail him a status update against the action plans discussed. However, if Nikhil does not hear from the client then what he would send the person a reminder after the coaching conversation especially in paid coaching conversations. In his emails, he captured the essence of the action plans expected**(E).**

- Nikhil would always mark a copy to himself, and If there's a target of follow-up on the 15th of this month, then he would drag and drop it into his Outlook calendar so that he monitored the follow-up rhythm. On the 15th day when Nikhil saw a popup and the client had not mailed in so far, he often picked that pop up or that Outlook mail, and he would forward the mail to the client asking for a status update. His often line was 'Hey! What's happening here? Do you want to send me a line on this? This for Nikhil was following up after the coaching conversation was over. Evaluate involves asking those questions afterward as well **(E)**.

- During every conversation, Nikhil would review the status of the past action plans and then only proceed to the next goal**(E).**

- In this case study, Nikhil has moved from Seeking information to Evaluate and application of action plans. We have in this process traversed through Seek, Observe, Listen, Value-add and Evaluate.

- Most of the 'Evaluate' steps could be substituted with the utility of the Learning Diary from Stimulus. This would shift ownership of all action plans and follow-up to the client. The best part is that the Coach could view status and generate reports as required from the tool.

Is there a template for the initial 1 X 1 Coaching summary?

Have a suggested template with specific lines including questions the Coach could ask the client. It is attached below:

INITIAL COACHING SUMMARY

Coachee:	Coach:	Date: Time:
Strengths: •	**Opportunities:** •	
Goals for the Project (with priorities): **Contractual obligations:**		
Area discussed during the recent Coaching Session: •		
Next Action Plans:	**Next Follow-up Schedule:**	

SOLVE© – THE COACHING MODEL:

SOLVE© involves five steps to engage in a Coaching conversation:

Step 1: *Seek* to prepare

- Gather as much background information as possible.
- Collect relevant data before engaging in the first coaching conversation

Step 2: *Observe*, and ask for the *outcome*

- Let the client speak.
- Ask for permission to coach, thank, clear space
  - o Explain the procedure – process, roles & responsibilities
- Clarify the protection – confidentiality, brief on coaching ethics

Establish the outcome in following terms:
  - o Ask for specific outcome – pin it down
  - o Ask for measure – how will you measure success?
  - o Check for motivation – what excites you about this goal? Or ask, how would it feel, when you reach your goal?
  - o Check if it is manageable — what are you committing for this goal?

Step 3: *Listen* for the message

- Practice reflective listening
- Establish the current situation (Ask & Listen)
  - o Ask a scaling question – on a scale of 10, where are you right now?
  - o What obstacles do you foresee?

o What are the challenges here?

Step 4: *Value-add* when you work-out solutions and create insights

- Establish the Options/Solutions. (Ask & Listen)
    - o In view of the gap, what specifically can help you?
    - o What options can you think of? Or what options do we have here?
    - o What would your role model suggest you here?
- Indicators of Success/Evaluation of Options
    - o In view of the outcome planned, shine some light on the each of the options
    - o What is appealing about this option?
    - o What will indicate success?
    - o What evidences will tell you the option is working?

- Blue Print the Achievement Strategy
    - o What actions do you intend to take now?
    - o What is your action plan?
    - o What do you intend to Start/Continue/Stop doing?
    - o What resources are required now?
    - o What support is required?

Step 5: *Evaluate* the actions

- Levers of Success/Love of 'To Be' state – What motivates you?
    - o Moving forward, what excites you about the outcome of these actions?
    - o How important is this achievement for you?
    - o What might derail you from your actions? How might you sustain your enthusiasm & energy?

- o What self-defeating behaviours might you encounter & how do you intend to keep yourself afloat?
- Executing the Actions
  - o Ask, when do you intend to start off?
  - o What checks and measures will be in place?
  - o Who will help you review your progress Vs plan?
  - o Is there someone whom you want to contract with?

How could a sponsor follow-up on Coaching Effectiveness? Is there a template recommended?

Attached is a template which evaluates behavioral change. The first part is filled by the client. The second part could be optionally filled in by the sponsor or the client's supervisor if viable as per the coaching contract.

Coaching Evaluation Form

Name of Client:
Name of the Intervention (if applicable):
Instructions: -
1. The first part of the form must be filled by the Client
2. The second part of the form is optional and must be filled by the Sponsor or Supervisor (if permitted by the coaching contract)
3. Please circle the answer of your choice.

Part 1: - To be filled by the Client

Parameters	Scales			
	4	3	2	1
1. Have you gone through the discussion notes and Coaching summary again?	Referred whenever I had doubt	Referred sometimes when I had a doubt	Referred once or twice	Not at all
2. Did the 1 X 1 conversation fulfil your objectives?	Yes, fulfilled all the objectives	Fulfilled most of the objectives	Fulfilled half of the objectives	Not at all
3. Have you found the acquired inputs from the Coaching program relevant to your job?	Relevant & implement able	Relevant & may be implement able	Relevant but not implementable	Not at all relevant to the job
4. Have you been able to apply the acquired skills to your job?	Could use two or three skills in my job	Could use only one skill in my job.	Has made me aware of self/areas of improvement	Not at all

SOLVE

5. Have the acquired skills from various Coaching conversations met your expectations?	Exceeded my expectations	Met my expectations to a large extent	Could have been better	Did not meet my expectations at all
6. Have these conversations helped you in your personal life?	Could use two or three skills in my day to day life.	Could use only one skill in my day to day life.	Has made me aware of self/areas of improvement	Not at all
7. Have you been able to implement your Action Plans?	More than 75% of it	Around 50% of it	25% of it	Not at all

8. Cite an example where you have been able to implement the acquired skills in your job.

_____
_____
_____
_____
_____

9. What barriers, if any, have you encountered that have prevented you from using skills or knowledge acquired by these coaching conversations?

_____
_____
_____
_____
_____

Client's Signature

2 Of 3

103

Part 2: - To be answered by the Supervisor / HR/ Sponsor in the presence of the Participant (optional – based on Client's discretion and Coaching contract)

Parameters	Scales			
	4	3	2	1
1. Have the coaching conversations helped the individual to apply newly acquired skills?	Could use two or three skills in the job.	Could use only one skill in the job.	Has made him aware of self/areas of improvem ent	Not at all
2. Does the individual use the acquired skills frequently?	Most of the time	Occasionall y	Rarely	Not at all
3. Do you believe that the organisation is benefiting from the acquired skills of the individual?	Strongly agree	Agree	Disagree	Strongly disagree
4. Has the individual implemented his / her Action Plans?	More than 75% of it	Around 50% of it	25% of it	Not at all

5. Identify any specific ON – THE – JOB accomplishments / improvement in the individual that you can link with these coaching conversations.

_____
_____
_____
_____
_____

Client's signature   Supervisor's Signature

Summary:

1. Managers often don't know how to coach. Teach them the simple approach of SOLVE©.
2. Use the structure and vision or purpose of SOLVE©.
3. Trained 'Helpers' Ask more than Tell. This engages our clients and involves them in the problem-solving process.
4. The solutions should come from the client. This ensures ownership and accountability to action plans.
5. Reflective listening skills take practice.
6. People often backslide after great 1 X 1s unless the action plans are clearly articulated, and ownership fixed.
7. Follow-up is the 'Coaches' responsibility, while you may hold the client accountable for owning his action plans. Use technology to do this best.

Nikhil's contribution to you:

Use the coaching summary and follow-up template to show actual behavioral change and justify the ROI for Coaching

BIG IDEA 9 - SOLVE© IN CONSULTING – THE RIGHT PEOPLE MATTER

Sometimes it is an individual approaching you at a personal capacity and asking for help. At other times, this may be a client wanting help to solve a business challenge. Many experts have attempted to differentiate the two into Coaching and Consulting. In practice, there is a lot of overlap and similarity. While Coaching is meant to be client-centric, Consulting is focused on the problem. In practice, all Coaching and Consulting is focused on the client and is an intervention to solve his or her real problems.

SOLVE© is a great model, which could be used in consulting and coaching.

Consequences of poor Consulting:

- Poor solution – This happens mostly when a Consultant chooses what has worked for him rather than his client's real interest.

- Lack of real commitment from clients – Often due to excessive advising.

- Incomprehensible language and complex solutions – Many Consultants are experts and provide solutions which are understood by experts but not by lay persons or business folks.

- Inability to show ROI and think like the business. Consultants looking to maximize billing from a client do not look for low-cost solutions or even justify the return from the spend.

- Many of the solutions have built-in fees, so investors are not even aware of the costs. In the end, high fees can eventually erode the future performance of the business.

- Selling what clients want, not what the client needs. Rather than provide solutions that meet a client's objective, a self-interested consultant may sell what the client asks for. The sales process is made more comfortable and more efficient for the consultant by recommending solutions to the client that the consultant knows the client will buy, even if they are not in the client's best interest. As a result, those investors who are sold products that appeal to their emotions might end up with solutions that are, inappropriate. Their investments are not aligned with their long-term objectives, which might result in too much risk.

- A Consultant is expected to be a specialist. They are expected to have substantial domain exposure and knowledge. Many people have the mistaken belief that consultants spend most of their day doing research and searching for ideas for their clients. Most consultants spend little time on research and more time on marketing, business development, client service, and administration. Pressed for time, they might not do a thorough analysis of the solutions they are recommending. Knowledge and understanding vary widely from consultant to consultant. Some are very knowledgeable and exceptionally competent when providing advice to their clients, and others are not. Some consultants might believe they are doing the right thing for their clients and not even realize that they are not. This poor consulting includes the following:

o Not fully understanding solutions they recommend

o Overconfidence

o Momentum solution – suggesting what's hot

o A poorly constructed solution as a cumulative result of bad advice. Often solutions are too complicated to understand — this could mean that risks are not apparent. They may become challenging to manage, and decisions cannot be made with confidence.

- The bottom line - Bad advice frequently results in poor performance or loss of money for clients. When choosing a consultant (or evaluating the one you have), stay alert for clues that might indicate that the consultant is not working in your best interest or is not as competent as you would like. After all, it's your money. If you're not happy with how you're being advised, it could pay to take it elsewhere.

Case - Study: Nikhil's experience conducting a workshop on Consulting Skills:

Nikhil was hired recently to train Consultants on 'Advanced Consulting skills.' After some study of the industry, he built some case studies from parallel industries. He picked up a great model and decided to run the session. He taught them things they already knew. They spent three days together and did not have too many aha moments or real take-aways. Nikhil was internally unhappy. The client organization was okay but did not specifically comment. The program went well and got some good feedback on the course rating scale. Yet Nikhil knew that he was not happy. He got his billing. There was a tick in the box, but no real change. Most of us are familiar with cases like these in Consulting.

We at Stimulus Consulting (my organization) attempted to guide Nikhil and discussed what went right and what could have gone better. With the learnings, we decided to do another project with the same Consulting house.

The client and context were the same – A global ERP Consulting Organization. Nikhil was hired to train consultants and make them better. These guys were veterans in ERP Consulting and senior folks. They had been there, done that. They already knew how to consult, but our task was to make them better Consultants, and we decided to use SOLVE©. We looked at a real-world case study where they could apply SOLVE©.

Within the case-study -   Seek in SOLVE©

We co-created a business simulation which followed these steps:

- The participants were asked to play their role as consultants. The client stakeholders and our team decided to play clients.
- It all started with the client sending a little e-mail stating the requirement. Oftentimes in the consulting industry, this is precisely how it all begins. The consultant receives an e-mail which is like a two liner or four-line e-mail.
- After the client sent this e-mail and the consultant read this e-mail, the consultant, internally shared this with his team.
- The consultant and his team dug up history and went through past documents since this was a repeat client,

there was a lot of history which was available within the organization.

- The consultants also searched online for publicly available data and did some quick R & D. They also evaluated social media space where they could get more information about the client and the need that was initially expressed.
- As part of Seek, the Consultant went one step behind to understand the problem.
- He also made a quick call to get an initial overview from the client. Problem identification was the task at hand. The consultant asked a couple of more questions to understand the problem at a very superficial level.
- The consultant continued to ask questions. He wanted to know if they wanted a solution or were they testing the waters.
- To understand change readiness, the client representative was asked – 'when do you want to do this?' Or 'what are the kind of resources you're willing to commit to it?' etc.
- In all consulting engagements, it's crucial that the consultant can ask and get a feel of how deep the problem is and how much is the client willing to commit to it.
- During the initial call, the consultant also asked for what the role is and what is the expectation of both parties. After clarifying all this, the consultant fixed a mutually convenient time to meet. He also asked if he could meet the actual stakeholders so that he could understand the needs at a deeper level.
- Nikhil realized that good consultant always try to meet the MAN (person with money, authority, and need). All of this was part of Seek.
- The great idea was to have an NDA (Non-disclosure agreement) in place early so that the client could be fully transparent with his need and would not hold back any part of the relevant information. The Consultant quickly

initiated a draft NDA so that this was handled before the client meeting.

- Before the scheduled meeting, the consultant in this simulation went back and spoke to his internal team. He shared the data that was gathered in the initial contact from the client. There were a couple of more clarifying questions that his team members asked the consultant and the consultant had not asked the client. So, the consultant picked up the call again and asked some of these essential questions, so that they could go prepared for the meeting.

Within the case-study -   Observe/Outcome in SOLVE©

- In the Observe / Outcome phase, the consultants put together a balanced team, which was constituted in such a way that the competencies the client were looking for, could be best served by these consultants. They carefully put together a team which had the right balance of competencies.
- They met people who were the actual stakeholders. These client representatives had the authority, they understood the need, and they also had access to funds and budgets.
- In the initial contact as part of 'Observe / Outcome' the consultant, shook hands, greeted and attempted to build rapport.
- After the initial social conversation and social grace, the client was thanked for bringing this requirement to their team.
- The Consultants started with summarizing the need expressed so far. They then asked the client to share a little more perspective on the need, the genesis of this need and any other relevant information.
- The consultant now asked more open questions to understand the need at a deeper level. The consultant

started with open questions, moved to closed questions, then summarized to say "Is this your requirement? If we give the solution would that fix the problem?".

- The Consultant asked the client how they would measure the success of this project. Nikhil found this an interesting question and rightly timed.
- All of this was the part of 'Observe / Outcome,' and there is a small part of Listen also which was exhibited at this stage.

Within the case-study -   Listen in SOLVE©

- After understanding the problem statement and getting the entire picture so far, the consultants summarized their understanding back to the client.
- Nikhil noticed that he was actively into the Listen stage. We were still vacillating between asking questions and listening (Observe and listen phases). These two phases work in tandem in consulting.
- Through the 'Observe / Outcome' phase, the consultant attempted to get to the need behind the need. He wanted to identify the basis for this requirement coming in.
- The consultants also attempted to find out what was really happening and what was tried so far.
- Nikhil made a note of some interesting questions which included - "What kind of resources are they willing to commit? How much money are they willing to invest? How deep is this project? Do we have senior leadership sign off? What are the contractual terms?"
- These requirements were agreed on, and this entire exploration that the consultant did would mark the end of the listen phase.
- After the consultant went back to the organization with those tangible needs, he shared what was found out. The consultants grouped with their colleagues in a meeting

room. The Practice Lead attempted to understand the requirement. The requirement was laid out on a large piece of paper or a whiteboard. The different elements of the requirement were discussed. A lot of questions were asked to the group of consultants to understand their real understanding of the client challenge. All of this happened internally.

- After a lot of discussions, tasks were divided between the consultants so that they pitch in to build a proposal. The first cut of an internal proposal was developed.

- In this process, they realized in some cases there was a need to gather more requirements. All these requirements may lead to some additional questions to be asked to the client. If there is a need, then these questions were also asked or clarified over a call.

- There was a lot of data gathering and analysis which was done at this stage. The real requirement was gathered from the customer. Internal capabilities were captured, and a lot of past work done was also utilized, and that data was also merged here. Goals and priorities were clearly articulated. There were plans made and accountability defined for each part of the deliverables.

- Internal searches continued around: "What kind of resources do we need? How many resources in man-days do we need for this project? What is the kind of an estimation that we need? All of this was incorporated into the proposal.

- The proposal was internally brainstormed, shared and finally approved internally so that it could be presented to the client.

- The proposal was mailed to the client with a request for schedule to meet.

- The consultant or the single point of contact (SPOC) asked the client for another appointment and sought time for the Consultant and relevant team members to meet the steering committee and present the proposal.

Within the case-study -   Value-add in SOLVE©

- The proposal was presented with as many granular details, timeline, etc. While at the presentation, more details were shared than what was in the proposal. The Consultant's expertise with other similar projects was also discussed.

- All client questions were answered.

- An extension to this meeting was a separate meeting where there was a detailed negotiation of commercial terms and deliverables. This meeting often happens with the commercial team's participation.

- When the consultant makes this conversation of offering the solution, this is the stage of Value-add.

- The consultant also asked, what else can he do and how can the client derive more value Additional features which the client may find useful were also discussed.

- The past exposure of the Consultant and his expertise was demonstrated. Questions to the client at this stage included facets the client never thought about earlier. The questions were based on the past work done by the consultant. These were not suggestions, just questions. There were questions around "How could we quickly achieving the learning curve?" Have you thought about...". Nikhil thought that these questions in some sense were suggestive. He quickly backed off when he realized that this was Consulting.

- They spoke about solutions which were not thought by the client. If the client asked for A and B, sometimes they missed C.

- An interesting question Nikhil found was around identifying the stumbling blocks and obstacles early. The Consultant asked, "What might derail us from our plans?"

- The consultant brought a new angle to the table. He said "Very often in a large ERP consulting situation there is a need for change management. You can easily do an ERP implementation. However, the struggle is getting the internal folks in the organization actually to adapt and move to the new system". They concluded that there was a big need for change management and training, which had to be included in the scope.

- The consultant based on his past exposure said that most of his past clients in similar space had ABC as a need, which was not expressed by the client. The client was then asked, "do you see this as a struggle?". He also asked if the client saw a need for a specific report, which was missed out. The client had also not considered a need to sync or back-up his data. There was also a need for movement between a legacy system to the current conventional system which was being proposed. There's a lot of past in the consultant's knowledge repository. All of this is utilized, discussed and finally, we have a plan in place saying this is what we will do. All of this is part of Value-add stage of V in SOLVE©.

Within the case-study -   Evaluate in SOLVE©

- Nikhil realized that in a consulting engagement, there isn't a clear differentiation or a demarcation between each of these steps in **SOLVE©**. The boundaries are fuzzy.
- Nikhil wanted to see the engagement so far from the client's point of view and evaluate how the solution worked for him. He asked the consultant "if I did all of this would that resolve the client problem? Would this be the complete solution we are looking for? How do we place ourselves in the client shoes post implementation and ask if the project was successful?"
- Within the simulation, Nikhil learned about some best practices used by ERP consultants, which was also applicable to others. During the implementation stage, the consultants got frequent sign-offs from the client at different stages, so that the solution confirmed to the

requirement initially stated. This also helped the consultants minimize re-work. The learning Nikhil achieved was to get a signoff from the client at each smaller toll-gate or micro stage.

- This stage is filled with enhanced activity, progress and change requests. The consultant had already estimated 10-15% of the effort time towards change requests. The big ones were separately classified as scope changes and were negotiated at an additional cost.

- The Consultant also monitored and measured progress against time and deliverables. There was also feedback taken at different points. Some feedback was incorporated into future release versions. To do this, the Client was asked to identify one individual who would administratively review progress Vs. plan. This enabled one sign-off for the consultant, rather than multiple influencers.

- All of this was part of the Evaluate stage. However, Nikhil realized that in the end, having a complete 'release or installation' and a 'go-live' was not the end of the project. The clients would continue to need support. In the simulation, evaluate continued into hand-holding and providing support as required.

- There is a stage where the project terminates, which means this project is done and over with. There are final steps of signing off in commercial closure which also happens. However, the consultant supports all the way here and beyond.

Nikhil decided to go back to the team he did a shoddy job with. He decided to do a review and share what was successful and what were the learnings from the project. These learnings were documented and discussed with his internal team. They also shared some action plans with the client. He decided to provide continued support.

Nikhil learned that this could happen for a year in a large ERP project based on contractual terms. However, the relationship had to be maintained. Often the relationship is maintained for over three years when the client chooses to go for the next upgrade or service. Nikhil decided to go back to all his clients to check if they required any support. His focus was "How is that approach going on? Is there any other support that they need?" Nikhil realized that this continued offer of help and support in a Consulting engagement brought him more work. He did not need a business development team if he did this part right! He realized that he was in the business of 'relationship marketing' His focus shifted from 'acquiring clients and servicing their requirements' to 'keeping them for life' using **SOLVE**©.

SOLVE© – THE CONSULTING MODEL:

SOLVE© involves five steps to engage in a Consulting conversation:

Step 1: *Seek* to prepare

- Gather as much background information as possible.
- Collect relevant data before engaging in the first conversation
- Explain the procedure – process, roles & responsibilities
    o Clarify the protection – Confidentiality / NDA– *if relevant*

Step 2: *Observe* and ask for the outcome

- Summarize the need expressed so far and ask the client to provide more information.
- Establish the Outcome in following terms:
    o Ask for specific outcome – pin it down
    o Ask for measure – how will you measure success of this project?
    o Check for motivation –, How would it feel, when you reach your goal?
    o Check if it is manageable – ask the client to clarify their commitment – what are you committing for this goal?

Step 3: *Listen* for the message

- Practice reflective listening
- Establish the Current situation (Ask & Listen)
    o What are the challenges here?

Step 4: *Value-add* when you work solutions

- Establish Options/Solutions. (Ask & Listen)
  - o In view of the gap, what specifically can help you?
  - o What options can you think of? Or what options do we have here?
- Indicators of Success/Evaluation of Options
  - o In view of the outcome planned, let us shine some light on each of the options.
  - o What is appealing about this option?
  - o What will indicate success?
  - o What evidences will tell you the option is working?
  - o What might derail you from your actions? How might you sustain your enthusiasm & energy?
- Blue Print the Achievement Strategy
  - o What actions do you intend to take now?
  - o What are your action plans?
  - o What do you intend to Start/Continue/Stop doing?
  - o What resources are required now?
  - o What support is required?

Step 5: *Evaluate* the actions

- Levers of Success / Love of 'To Be' state – What motivates you?
  - • Moving forward, what excites you about the outcome of these actions?
  - • How important is this achievement for you?
  - • What self-defeating behaviours might you encounter?
- Executing the Actions
  - • Ask, when do you intend to start off?
  - • What checks and measures will be in place?

- Who will help you review your progress Vs plan?
- Is there someone whom you want to contract with?

Summary:

1. Dig up history, go through past documents, ask questions before the first meeting.
2. Fix a meeting with the MAN (person with Money Authority and Need)
3. Send the right people to meetings - Carefully put together a team which has the right balance of competencies.
4. Plan and list your questions.
5. Showcase and use your past expertise (unlike Coaching)
6. For large projects, identify a SPOC (Single point of contact). Define responsibilities, and accountability for key tasks. Discuss an escalation matrix if appropriate.
7. Get to the need behind the need
8. Questions at the Value-add stage should include facets the client never thought about earlier
9. Constantly monitor and measure progress against time and deliverables.
10. Shift your focus from 'acquiring clients and servicing their requirements' to 'keeping them for life', offering genuine support.

Nikhil's realization - Right people matter:

> As a consultant, constitute a team with the right subject matter expertise. This matters in consulting. From the client side, always meet the MAN – person with money, authority and need.

BIG IDEA 10 - SOLVE© REQUIRES A CULTURE SHIFT. IT IS ABOUT A MINDSET

How does one take this forward into daily application?

SOLVE© needs to be a template and a formula which everyone needs to bear in mind when you are in any interaction. This is not only for consultants and coaches but also for parents. This is for any peer, a leader or a follower. This is for anyone who is attempting to solve a problem. Would like it if all individuals bear the template of **SOLVE**© which is seek, observe, listen, value-add and evaluate in their mind and they should follow these steps.

Using **SOLVE**©, a lot of situations will lead to solutions rather than lead to problems in daily application. One needs to seek information before jumping into action. We need to let others talk and look at where others are going first. We need to listen to them. We need to create insights, discuss options and arrive at solutions which are better than the obvious. We need to create those insights. All solutions need to be evaluated, to ensure that the solutions please the original intent. We need to confirm that this is to the Client's satisfaction and then we need to ensure that this is applied long term. This is a template which needs to be and can be applied in most daily situations.

Just common sense put into a model, with a realization that common sense is not so common. While we know it, we still do not do our pre-work before meetings; we do not let others speak first; we are poor at listening; we enforce our methods; we do not check after fixing issues. Issues we see everywhere could be fixed if this common sense becomes common application.

Is SOLVE© applicable to children?

Remember my daughter wanting to go through multiple career paths. Children often have whims and fancies, when they are tiny. Many want to become teachers. Many of them do it if they have seen some impressive teachers. Lots of boys want to become pilots, doctors, engineers. The society conditions them, and they all have these little aspirations. The exciting part though is that aspirations change over a period. What you are sure of, is that they are unsure in most cases. Being the proud parent of two great children, we realized that our kids did not know what they wanted to do. Their choices changed very often. My wife and I decided to get our kids to take up multiple aptitude tests at a recognized center, followed by career counseling. Seeking this input early was part of the first step of SOLVE©. We did a complete aptitude test series which lasted for about four to five hours. Multiple aptitudes were checked. After getting all that information, there was an interview with an external counselor from the center. They built a detailed report for both our kids. Now having this helped me make a conversation with my kids concerning what career choices they considered. The tests were not conclusive since there were at least three or four different directions suggested. We threw these options on the table. Remember my daughter asking me about each of these careers since her worldly exposure was limited. We asked her what appealed to her and her logic. We also asked her why some of the choices did not appeal to her. We let her talk and listened to her. We got her thinking about perspectives she had not considered before and hardships she had not known. After she zeroed in on her choice, we reaffirmed her commitment by bringing up the obstacles she could face and the challenges she may need to fight. We asked her if she was still for it. When the opportunity came, she took that pre-decided career path. Very proud to see her commitment to the course she chose. A path which is challenging and hard. Thanks to **SOLVE**©.

Have seen a lot of parents tell their kids "I want to die seeing you as an engineer or to seeing you as a doctor (often happens in India)." We rub our goals on them. The result of this is that a lot of their dreams are not out in the open. Our task as parents is to unlock that hidden potential in kids. **SOLVE**© therefore, is a great model to apply, especially with kids.

What is the advice when we use this at home?

A critical component of **SOLVE**© is to be dispassionate. We need to focus on behaviors and not the person. We need to work with evidence which includes externally observable behaviors or actions.

What can hinder or hamper this approach is emotions. The tricky part for all parents, kids, and others in a home context is to let the emotions out. It's therefore difficult to keep it objective. It is critical that one keeps the emotion away, listens logically, rationally, uses data and focuses on facts to proceed in any direction. The most critical part is to hold back that emotion and to keep it objective.

Where could SOLVE© fail?

Can think of a few instances where **SOLVE©** may not be successful. A lot of those are pointing to poor application. However, let me go through it one by one.

- The first one is incorrect prognosis.

  o A lot of us do not seek enough information before we jump in. Returning to my kids' example, if we only analyzed what do our children want. Is it just an engineer or doctor? Doing an aptitude test is seeking that data. The incorrect prognosis could lead in different directions.

  o In a corporate context, paradigms act as filters for leaders and managers. Paradigms are a set of rules which govern the way we think and act. This results in managers and leaders taking up beaten paths. They are limited by their existing paradigm that they're not thinking beyond their set of rules which act as boundaries. The message is to go beyond and dig deeper to find out what is happening.

  o We ask all our leaders to be data-oriented, attempting to use numbers. However, my message is to look beyond the numbers and focus on the stories behind the numbers. Focus on the behaviors which contribute to the numbers. We realize that we cannot change numbers, but we can change behaviors, which in turn influences the numbers. In a business context, understand what behavior is contributing to numbers and let's be objective in working on the behaviors which are evidenced which are visible and observable. Working with all of this is very critical to keep the system right. All these contribute to incorrect prognosis.

- The second reason why **SOLVE**$^©$ could fail is if the client lacks the will.
  o Often we've been in coaching and consulting situations where the individual does not have the willingness to change.
  o Nikhil described a situation he faced. He was Helping a senior leader who was nominated by his boss to attend this program. He noticed that he seemed very supportive and wanted to be there. He never changed that down the interactions, but over time, Nikhil realized that his schedules were not being adhered to. If there was a customer visit or something, that got prioritized over their conversation. He realized that there was no real will in that person to go through this process. **SOLVE**$^©$ can fail if there is no willingness in the individual to push things into the application. Nikhil concluded that an important task for all 'Helpers' would be to evaluate willingness and commitment before you apply **SOLVE**$^©$. We need to ensure that they have the will to apply; that this is really what they want, and they're not forced into this conversation (sometimes by their bosses).
- The senior leaders/supervisors need to be committed beyond the budget they earmark for an intervention.
  o Nikhil had this large organization which wanted a performance management system. After a lot of discussion with the functional leaders and gathering needs, Nikhil built a customized Performance Management system for them consuming a lot of time and effort. He also got paid handsomely for the effort. The senior leader was initially very open and contributed his inputs into the approach. He also chaired the meeting and ensured his managers complied with requirements. Later, Nikhil realized that the senior leaders just wanted a tick in the box

because they wanted to ensure that there was a system in place. They were not committed to putting this into organization-wide practice. They chose to exempt themselves from the new system. They only wanted levels below them to be assessed using the new method. As anyone could guess, the system died a slow death.

- The next reason why **SOLVE**© could fail is the organizational culture and specifically the client's supervisor or the boss not being supportive beyond lip service.
  - o We make great action plans in any coaching or consulting conversations. However, once people go back, they are up against a specific environment. Bosses are responsible for creating that environment and the culture. The leader creates this environment where Coaching related action plans survive or die. A lot of followers who have the right intent and the right solutions are not able to apply because the environment does not permit them to apply it.
  - o Remember one organization I visited. The Senior-most leader received me, and I was asked to follow him. On the way to his room, as he was walking, I noticed that there was someone who came out to carry his bag. Someone else also offered to carry my bag, which I politely refused. Noticed that every employee had a great deal of reverence for this man. He was also very autocratic with his style and was known to hire and fire. We had very high attrition levels and mass exodus. He thought everyone else was to blame.
  - o During the Helping engagement with his Direct reports, we co-created and built a lot of action plans. Later, we realized that he was the bottleneck. He had a certain approach. The culture he created just did not let them lead effectively, the way they would have liked them to or the way they committed to me

that they would do. The result was every time I went back I saw new faces among the senior leaders. There was a lot of attrition. Realized that 'culture eats our solutions for breakfast.' When I say that I believe that if we're not able to set the right culture, a lot of these action plans will not stick.

- Some of these interventions fail when a lot of leaders start advising from the word go. This is not only about leaders. There are also parents who do a lot of it.
  - Look at most parents who want to see their children succeed. They are always the first ones to advise. After a certain point, kids start resisting those same inputs. Parents need to hold back from advice. Similarly, Managers and young leaders notice that a lot of mistakes could be corrected by just simple logic. They are quick to advise. After a certain time, team members get conditioned to the inputs that they stop thinking and contributing. The most difficult part of the model is stopping oneself from telling and advising. A strong recommendation - 'develop the ask, don't tell habit' Can we all start asking and stop telling? We achieve the same outcomes with a higher commitment from our followers.
- 'Helpers' and Advisors of all kinds often let the participants or the clients go without creating any new insights.
  - They get them to do the stuff that clients come up with. A lot of times after going back the client feels that they did not arrive at any new solutions. In their words "The coach did not get me to think in a new direction. After I went to him or her, I did not get this new direction to work". This happens when the Helper has not created any new insights. He could do this sometimes by respectfully challenging the client. It is important

that we do not just let the client go away without creating that insight in his/ her mind. If we do not go beyond the obvious, **SOLVE**© could fail. This also means that the value-add in creating insights part was not effectively done.

- The last reason why I think among the many others why **SOLVE**© could fail is due to lack of follow up.
  o We've seen this to be the biggest cause, since we believe we have good people, with good intentions. Yet no change happens. Remember this large organization which wanted to have a key account management process, and we built this awesome process. We had this great technique to map an account. We captured client data and mapped the health of the client organization. We also co-defined the future of what will happen in that organization. We did all this together on paper. Remember doing this workshop in Singapore. However, when we went back six months later, we realized things were just the same, and things had not moved. We noticed the single largest reason why a lot of coaching and consulting interactions fail is because follow up is just not happening. Follow up as I mentioned earlier, is the Helpers' responsibility and without follow-up a lot of action plans slide back. Earlier we spoke about following up with kids when we correct their behavior. What we inspect, they respect!

Chapter Summary:

The different reasons for SOLVE© to fail:
- Incorrect prognosis.
- Lack of will/commitment in Client.
- The organizational culture or the Supervisor's culture not being supportive of action plans.
- A lot of telling which leaders and parents do.
- Letting people go without any new insights being created and additional value-add being contributed.
- Lack of follow up and remember 'what we inspect, they respect.'

My ask of you:

SOLVE© *requires a culture shift. It is not about a formula, it is about a mindset shift and a new culture in the making.*

Chapter Outline and Overview

Part One: Understanding the Overview

Big Idea 1: We can all 'Help' someone

There is always someone who comes to us and says "you got a minute? I have a challenge I want to discuss". As line Managers, leaders, coaches, consultants, parents, and untrained 'Helpers,' we all help others solve their problems. **SOLVE**$^{©}$ provides a tried and tested approach for anyone to help Solve issues. **SOLVE**$^{©}$ could be used as a thumb-rule and a process to make 1 X 1 problem-solving conversations.

As a Manager, historically I've been responsible for results. However, my approach has changed, now, thanks to all my learning over the period. **SOLVE**$^{©}$ is an approach that any Helper can pick-up and use as a thumb-rule for any 1X1! You don't need to be certified or credentialed to help others!

Big Idea 2: SOLVE$^{©}$ a thumb-rule for Coaching and Consulting

There have been times when we have been underprepared to handle a question from someone. Very often we do not stop to think about the personal style of the other person (Let us call him the client from now on). This model is applicable in our personal and professional lives. Citing a personal situation - When handling children, we are quick to advise and tell them. We instruct from the word go. Citing a professional situation - Many Coaching models recommend that you do not suggest. In the interest of being nice, we often do not move people into action plans. We tell our followers many things. We forget to follow-up, and we've seen it all go back to square one. **SOLVE**$^{©}$ uses these situations to build a model usable in most problem-solving situations. The foundation stones on which this model is built are S- Seek; O-Observe and Outcome; L – Listen; V- Value-add & E – Evaluate. Coaches, Consultants, and leaders – internalize these to have that quick chat!

Part Two: The Model

Big Idea 3: Seek the data, find out the story behind the numbers

Process Step 1: Seek to prepare and gather information

Preparation and gathering information before any engagement is critical. Without this first step, we've seen many Helpers work in the wrong direction. First impressions are not always right!

Some of the pre-work could include assessing history, behavioral patterns, etc. before they attempt to solve any issue. Without knowledge/information, the solution may not fit the client.

We cannot change numbers, and we can only influence behaviors. Get the numbers as part of Seek, however, find out behaviors that lead to numbers and then it will look manageable.

Big Idea 4: Observe, define the Outcome and the real need behind the need

Process Step 2: Observe and ask, define the outcome

In the first part of an interaction and most other personal situations, dumb is smart. Good to observe and assess behavioral patterns, ask questions and gather symptoms before we move to problem resolution.

Observation becomes one of the essential qualities of a Helper. During the initial phase of interaction with the client, the Helper must observe the client mood and obvious signs of discontent. See what the client is trying to say, what he/she is arriving at. Allow him or her to talk and vent. Do you let them speak? Do we believe that dumb is smart?

One should always start a conversation on a participative mode. It is critical that every Helper starts in a stage of observation where we understand the problem before we prescribe a solution. 'O' also represents the outcome. The Helper needs to at this stage define the outcome or the goal for the conversation.

Often what the client initially seeks, is not what he needs. Ask questions, get to the need behind the need. Define the real outcome.

Big Idea 5 – Be a reflective listener

Process Step 3: Listen for the message.

How often have we told someone 'you did not understand!' Beyond listening to the words spoken, a Helper should have the skill to filter the words for the core message. An upset client can say things that are not relevant to the current situation. Hence understanding and extracting the real issue from a heap of unrelated data becomes crucial in resolving the issue and all the facts. The practice of reflective listening shows that you understand the client. Reflectively listen and get them to feel understood!

When you reflect, what you say must always be shorter than what the speaker said!

Big Idea 6 – When you Value-add, create insights, get the client to think new solutions

Process Step 4: Value-add when you create new insights to build solutions

Value-add includes discussing the challenge, goal, problem or the situation and seeking options. It involves creating insights in the client's mind so that the person can do new things and think in new directions which the person had not thought of so far. This step aims to exceed the client's expectation by thinking about those new solutions or new directions. Before the client approaching the Helper, the client may not have thought about this new direction. However, after the conversation, the individual sees this as great new way.

Ask powerful questions, so that you can unlock the client's hidden potential and draw out those insights. Help them think their solutions, which were not in their radar earlier.

Big Idea 7 – Ensure you Evaluate. What you inspect, they respect.

Process Step 5: Evaluate the actions

One common mistake Helpers make, is to assume that client is happy after the conversation. We have learned the hard way, that majority of the attrition in most corporates is due to the managers. Hence the need to check that the Client is happy with the resolution of the problem he faced. Feedback, therefore, is essential to be recorded from the Client. Post the dialogue we also need to follow-up and ensure that the action plans discussed are being followed. What we inspect, they respect. Be it at home or work.

These steps of re-confirmation and follow-up are an integral part of the 'Evaluate' phase. Follow-up is the Helper's responsibility!

Use technology to do this. Use a shared tool where the Coach and Client have visibility.

Part Three: Application and Tips

Big Idea 8 - SOLVE© in Coaching – measure and monitor change

As a leader or as a professional Coach, we often realise that we can contribute to someone's performance and help them grow. **SOLVE©** is a great Coaching model which provides the steps for a new Coach and also as a guide for practicing coaches . It acts as a thumb-rule in the process of Coaching.

Use the coaching summary and follow-up template to show actual behavioral change and justify the ROI for Coaching.

Big Idea 9 - SOLVE© in Consulting – Right people matter

Sometimes it is an individual approaching you at a personal capacity and asking for help. At other times, this may be a client wanting help to solve a business challenge. Many experts have attempted to differentiate the two into Coaching and Consulting. In practice, there is a lot of overlap and similarity. While Coaching is meant to be client-centric, Consulting is focused on the problem. In practice, all Coaching and Consulting is focused on the client and is an intervention to solve his or her real problems.

As a consultant, constitute a team with the right subject matter expertise. This matters in consulting. From the client side, always meet the MAN – a person with money, authority, and need.

Big Idea 10 - SOLVE© requires a culture shift. It is not about a formula, and it's about a mindset.
Conclusion: Action planning and Summary

After every interaction, it would be prudent for the Helper to ask himself or herself if he/she followed the **SOLVE©** process. Evaluating needle movements on performance, organizational measurements on customer engagement or employee engagement scores, etc., are all modes to evaluate the success of **SOLVE©**

The utility of the five steps Seek, Observe, Listen, Value-add and Evaluate leads to engagement and harmony in any work area or home. Encourage each of you to adapt **SOLVE©** and internalize it in your day to day dialogues and difficult conversations!

We have seen a unique opportunity for **SOLVE©** in large culture building project initiatives and see this as the future of Organizational Development (OD). A blended initiative which uses coaching and consulting along with facilitating and group coaching. We see this as a formula which can **SOLVE©** most Organizational dilemmas and can also accelerate growth.

SOLVE© requires a culture shift. It is not about a formula, and it is about a mindset shift and a new culture in the making.

ABOUT THE AUTHOR

Sunil George is the **Founder Director** of Stimulus Consulting (P) Ltd, has over 27 years of experience in Consulting and Organizational Development initiatives across a cross-section of industries.

In December 1996, he was nominated among the top 3 Human Resource Managers in India for the H & FS award for excellence in hospitality. In January 1997 he moved into Apex Training Services as a Trainer Consultant and was actively involved in customized Corporate Training in a variety of disciplines across the country. After completing his Masters in Psychology and an MBA, he works with some of the best of Corporate Houses across Asia-Pacific.

During Sep 2008, he was awarded for securing the highest average score across Essential Leadership Skills conducted by GE Global Learning. He is also a 'CBA' – Certified Behavioral Analyst and facilitates behavioral analysis using DiSC profiling.

He is an Assess International Certified Professional on Strategic Competency Modeling & Competency

Framework, Assess 360 Feedback and Development Centers. Areas of specialization include Consulting, Designing, developing & delivering various Organizational Development & People Development Solutions for corporates, Performance Management Systems, top-talent projects. Assessment Centers / Development Centers.

After being Crotonville Certified, he spends a large chunk of his time on Leadership projects across different GE businesses in the ASEAN Region .

As a member of the International Coach Federation, he is a Credentialed PCC (Professional Certified Coach) and does Executive Coaching at different levels.

With Ford Motor Company, he is a sixth year Coach and India Field Mentor on the Global Ford CEM project. Beyond Ford Motor Company, he has worked with various businesses of GE, SAP, Schneider Electric, Airbus, ZF, TE Connectivity, KPMG, ANZ, Capgemini, Intelenet, Katera, Glaxo SmithKline, U.B group, Titan, Standard Chartered Bank, Euro RSCG, Phillips, Deutsche Software, Seven Seas Dubai, NBC – Singapore, Precision Tech Services Colombo, Satyam Computers, Hindustan Levers, Robert Bosch, UL, Yahoo, Shell, Century Link, Walmart, GXS, Synopsys, Ness etc.

He has also been in customized interventions with some of our international partners in Singapore, Malaysia, UAE, Bahrain, Kuwait, Srilanka, Indonesia, Vietnam, Philippines, Thailand, and China.